Jungle
and Other Tales

True stories of historic counterintelligence operations

DUVAL A. EDWARDS

Jungle and Other Tales
True stories of historic counterintelligence operations
Copyright © 2008 Duval A. Edwards. All rights reserved. No part of this book may be reproduced or retransmitted in any form or by any means without the written permission of the publisher.

Published by Wheatmark™
610 East Delano Street, Suite 104, Tucson, Arizona 85705 U.S.A.
(888) 934-0888 ext. 3
www.wheatmark.com

ISBN: 978-1-58736-945-2
LCCN: 2007934999

*To the memories of
Both of my wives:
Cissy Jameson and Kay Kohara*

From the Author

THIS IS A COMPILATION of articles written before, after and when I was the editor of the *Golden Sphinx*, publication of the National Counter Intelligence Corps, which I started in 1948 naming it *The CIC Reporter*. Most of these articles are from sources known to me, or rewrites from submission of others.

As editor-in-chief of the *Golden Sphinx*, official publication of the National CIC Association, I received different stories from around the world, as CIC covered the globe, being stationed where it could service any of our troops and air force in the jungles of Burma and southeast Asia, or the jungles of New Guinea, the Philippines, even the middle east involving Iran which was a pathway to Russia for supplies. Enemy agents were widespread and only a handful of CIC agents were operating in the territory. CIC also covered the U.S., sharing work with the FBI and the Navy's ONI under an agreement outlining the jurisdiction of each.

But the FBI was confined mostly to continental U.S., though it had representatives in such places as the Philippines when CIC Headquarters reached there. The Navy's ONI was undermanned and CIC found itself doing some of ONI's job overseas such as inspecting the cargo on every ship landing in support of U.S. troops, and investigating every sailor on board.

When President Roosevelt had meetings with the leaders

of our Allies in the war with Germany and Japan, CIC agents were usually there guarding him against possible assassins. Even his wife, Eleanor, had the protection of CIC when she visited a number of hot spots around the world.

Contents

I	Biography: Duval A. Edwards	1
II	The Beginning	4
III	First CIC Unit in World War I	7
IV	Was the Army's Secret Service *Too* Secret?	10
V	First Gabardine CIC School: Chicago 1942	16
VI	Air Force Fights for Its Own CIC	20
VII	Manhattan Project: Special Agent Gleaves	24
VIII	The Afro-American Army and Race Riots	27
IX	Biak Jungle Tales	31
X	Harry L. Amerman	36
XI	Santa Rosa, Laguna de Bay	39
XII	Manhattan District CIC's *Astounding* Case	44
XIII	CIC in Alaska	50
XIV	CIC in New Zealand in WW2	55
XV	"Ohayo, Gozai Masu"	63
XVI	CIC Authors Hall of Fame	67
XVII	Chaos in Postwar Japan	74
XVIII	Richard Sakakida, Hero in War with Japan	78
XIX	The Story of the Security Intelligence Corps	83
XX	Japanese Fifth Column in the Philippines	88
XXI	Liberating Bataan and Corregidor	95
XXII	Where Were You X Years Ago?	101

XXIII	Sakakida Rescues 500	105
XXIV	Jerry A. Alajajian	109
XXV	Looking into the Past	115
XXVI	Muscle Shoals Case	119
XXVII	Anniston Hotel Case	121
XXVIII	Fort McClelland Nazi Mechanic	125
XXIX	Case of Airborne Death in Training	130
XXX	Some CIC Outstanding Cases	132
XXXI	How Deep Was the Great Depression?	137
XXXII	Cactus Jack Y Canon	142

I

Biography of a Former San Antonian: Duval A. Edwards

IN 1937 AT THE age of 21, Edwards became a Texas lawyer in San Antonio TX, practicing there with the Law Offices of State Senator Harry Hertzberg until Edwards entered the Army in 1941. Duval was born near Olla, Louisiana; but considers himself at least a Texas "shorthorn" as his father was a full Texas "longhorn" born in Brownsboro, Texas. As a hobo Duval came to Texas in 1932, [told in his Great Depression book] and has been a:

> shoeshine boy, soda jerker, amateur boxer, elephant water boy, door-to-door circular distributor, dishwasher, carhop, ditch digger, bookbindery worker, elevator operator, newspaper seller, surveyor's rodman, law office clerk, lawyer, credit manager, technical editor/writer for Prentice-Hall, claim adjuster for USF&G Insurance Co., bill collector—not necessarily in that order.

When in San Antonio after being admitted to the legal bar of Texas, he married Elizabeth 'Cissy' Jameson who died two years after the marriage, causing him to volunteer for the army. Not mentioned in that long list: four years in the Army as a Military Intelligence Special Agent in CIC [Counter Intelligence Corps], two years of which [1941-3] were in Southern states [Louisiana; Alabama; Mississippi, Georgia], two years [1944-45] in the Pacific [Sydney, Australia; Hollandia and Biak in Dutch New Guinea; Bougainville in Solomon Islands; Luzon in Philippines]. He was Special Agent in Charge with 41st CIC [41st Division] and 214th CIC [XIVth Corps]; his last CIC assignment: in 1945 with the 306th CIC [Sixth Army] in Philippines, in charge of counter-intelligence investigations within Sixth Army territory and participating in capturing over 5,000 enemy spies and collaborators. In Japan he did no work as reaching Kyoto with first troops found orders sending him home on points.

Postwar, in addition to technical writing and editing for Prentice-Hall, he has written and published: manual for claim adjusters and sub rogation attorneys in Texas; The Great Depression, about his struggles on the road looking for work in 1932; The Senator and the Runaway Teenager in the Great Depression, sequel to his Great Depression, history book titled Spy Catchers of the U.S. Army in the War with Japan; all revised and printed in one volume titled Short Horn Hobo: Son of the Great Depression. Editor and writer for Golden Sphinx, CIC veterans' national quarterly for 9 years [which he started in 1947]; he was coauthoring Japanese Soldiers in WW2 with native Texan and fellow CIC agent William A Owens [*This Stubborn Soil, Eye-Deep In Hell, Black Mutiny* (basis for *Amistad* movie), plus twelve others] until Owens' final illness. He has plans for a first novel with working title of *Louisiana Sub Culture*.

Now a citizen of Seattle, Washington, Edwards resided with his wife of 60 years, Kay [nee Kohara], retired pediatrician, who died at age 86 in November 2006. They have two children: daughter Lynn Edwards Fulghum, family physician married to Robert Fulghum, writer [*All I Really Need to Know, I Learned in Kindergarten*, etc]; and son Walter D Edwards, PhD, university professor and writer [*Modern Japan Through its Weddings*] at Tenri, Nara, Japan, married to Michiko [nee Fujita] — they are parents of Duval & Kay's only grandchildren: Gen Michael, Myra Sakiko, Karen Asuka.

II

The Beginning

When my first wife died, I was devastated. As she lay dying in my arms, her final and last words were, "Duval, I want you to marry again."

After a few months I decided to volunteer for the U.S. Army. I wrote to my draft board that I was ready, and that I was moving but would keep it appraised of my whereabouts. Shortly after that, a good friend and his wife dropped by San Antonio, picked me up and took me with them to Georgia, where he was going to work at Fort Benning as one of a crew who were writing the Occupational Specialists of different soldiers.

I roomed with them in Columbus GA, advising my draft board of my new address. In a couple of months I received my draft notice to enlist either back at Fort Sam Houston in San Antonio or in the fort in Atlanta GA. I selected Atlanta as it was nearest, and reported there within a week in June 1941.

The first thing I said to the clerk welcoming me was, "I am a lawyer. Can I be assigned to the Judge Advocates?"

"We have too many lawyers already," he replied. So he continued giving me an intelligence test and other things that had to be done to get me in the army. After a week at the Fort,

I was sent with a number of other enlistees to Camp Wheeler, an infantry training camp near Macon GA. I was assigned to a company in the 4th Battalion which was training to send and receive by Morse code. In about two weeks, I had gotten up to 22 words a minute on the equipment in front of me.

Alongside of me was another young lawyer from New Orleans LA, whom I liked and kept company with. We became good friends. Then we both were transferred to another company in the same battalion into a platoon with 47 lawyers and a preacher, all from the state of Tennessee. They were being trained for I and R work with the infantry. As I learned, the IR men were explorers and recognizance workers behind the lines of the enemy in battle, reporting back on what they had found to the intelligence authorities.

The subjects taught us was all about the various units in our army and their functions. About halfway through our 13 weeks training, I acquired a giant toothache and took time off to see the army dentists. After the initial exam I was told I had a rotten spot in my tooth and had to have it drilled out. The dentist explained they had no ether available but I must have the decay drilled out and the cavity filled; the dentist also stated, "If I pulled this tooth out, you would then have one below the minimum required for an officer of the army. What do you want to do, save the tooth or have it extracted?"

"Save it. I may be an officer some day."

So he began drilling while I did my best to endure the intense pain of the drilling without ether – and I succeeded, to my own surprise.

Near the end of our 13 weeks of training, we were told we would have to attend a lecture on sex. Too many cases of soldiers acquiring sexual diseases were reported. So we marched to a lecture hall where a Chaplain welcomed us. His opening remarks were, "Men, I am going to surprise you and keep this short. I'll tell you the story of Fido the dog whose favorite pastime was beating a railroad train across the tracks. Well, one day he was a little slow. The train engine cut off the end of his tail; he whipped around to see what had happened and his head was cut off. So men, don't ever lose your head over a little piece of tail." He was the most popular chaplain I ever ran into in the army.

III

First CIC Unit in World War I

In going through the memorabilia of our member John D. "Jack" Christine who died many years ago, his widow Betty came across this newspaper clipping that Jack had saved. She thoughtfully sent it along with a batch of photos to our Jim Marion for disposition. We thought this particular one fit right in with the reason for this section of Golden Sphinx.

Sound Familiar?

The laudatory story that accompanied the photo recounted that the first 50 agents of this new CIP [Corps of Intelligence Police] organized "against everybody's better judgment," reached France Nov. 1917: Military Police met them at the dock and promptly arrested them! They were then sent to AEF HQ and put to work digging latrines - until their orders finally arrived and they got out of the ditches and proceeded to do their work.

Wanted or not, the agents did such a good job capturing saboteurs, neutralizing German courier and communications lines, etc, that when the German Army collapsed in 1918, CIP's number had swelled to 450.

The CIP changed its name to CIC [Counter Intelligence Corps] in WW2 and went on to greater glories in neutralizing subversion in the Army and watchdogging the famed Manhattan Project.

The news story apparently came out because at Ft. Holabird, the CIC, "the granddaddy of modern military counter intelligence was celebrating its 50th anniversary."

From WW 2 On

Marshall M. Meyer of Baltimore was quoted by the paper as recalling "how some 250 CIC agents handling the security of Operation Overlord did their work so well, it was hours after the actual invasion began before Hitler himself would believe it was real and not a diversionary attack. "During the Battle of the Bulge, CIC agents worked night and day to block a plan by the top German master spy, Otto Skorzeny, to infiltrate handpicked Germans in American uniforms through the Allied lines.

"Our agents found out about his plan by the first day of the attack and within hours had alerted security units to set up an identification procedure that resulted in the arrest of virtually all the infiltrators."

CIC agents also distinguished themselves in non-combat areas, including Iceland where they captured three Germans sent to establish a weather station there.

In the Middle East, CIC furnished info on delicate problems involving our so called ally, Russia, and in Cairo an investigation of a suspected subversive led them into the crack-up of a huge gold smuggling ring.

Still at it in Korea

During the Korean conflict, CIC smashed a vast Chinese Communist espionage net and captured its leader known by his code name of "X-ray." In his pockets was a scrap of paper with a scribbled date, "15 September Inchon." On September 6, he had learned of our plan for the Inchon landing on the 15th, and admitted he was to have messaged the vital info the very day he was apprehended. CIC foiled what would have been a major attempt by the North Koreans to abort this victorious Inchon landing behind enemy lines.

The Evening' News concludes this overall report that covers three wars that CIC was in, with this pithy statement.

"Today it [CIC] is fighting in Vietnam. "

What will papers say on CIC in Vietnam?

IV

Was the Army's Secret Service *Too* Secret?

SP: Secrecy Psychosis, its occupational disease.

This is a revision of an article by Duval Edwards published in The CIC Reporter, *April 1948; it also was the first story published in* Duty, Valor and Honor *in 2006.*

A FEW WEEKS AFTER Pearl Harbor, one of U. S. Army's top generals phoned J. Edgar Hoover, FBI chief, saying "Edgar, we're scheduling a Top Secret meeting with top officers of our Allies. We want you to send some plain clothes agents to take care of its security."

Hoover's reply: "General, why don't you use your own plain clothes agents?"

The general: "My God! Do we have them?"

Hoover: "Since 1917, General!"

That in a nutshell explains a major problem for Army's expert spy catchers from the very beginning: not only to catch enemy agents bent on espionage, sabotage, etc., but also battle our own Army as only a few in 1941 knew of its own plainclothes Counter Intelligence Corps.

In 1941, to be accepted into this secret organization a soldier had to finish basic training, be at least 25 years old with an IQ of 120 or higher, and have a working knowledge of at least one foreign language, with experience in some form of investigations. Among some 1000 agents on duty January 1, 1942, the great majority were former lawyers, judges, FBI agents, police and private detectives, credit investigators, newspaper reporters, college professors -- in other words, mature, experienced adults, with backgrounds checked for loyalty, honesty and discretion.

Each new agent swore not to tell even closest relatives the existence of CIC and his connection to it. Forbidden to tell a spouse or parent caused many agents to suffer from a malady doctors couldn't diagnose, but which I've labeled "SP: Secrecy Psychosis, CIC's occupational disease."

For me, it started in summer of 1941 while eating dust in 13 weeks basic training in Camp Wheeler GA. While washing down our throats with peach sodas, my buddy confided he was asked by the PIO [Post Intelligence Officer] to join a secret intelligence outfit.

"What does it do?" I asked.

"I don't know exactly. All he said was it's called CIP, Corps of Intelligence Police. Its members sometimes wear civvies, and . . ."

I didn't hear the rest. Civilian clothes! Thinking of fatigues, Georgia dust, infantry pack and '03 rifle, I told my friend not to be bashful about applying.

Two days later, the PIO received my application and ordered me to his office at once. I arrived under personal escort of my worried company commander.

The PIO quizzed me intensely. Did my qualifications for CIP interest him? NO! He wanted to know how I had learned the name of the secret organization, and if any word of its existence had leaked to others. Such secrecy impressed me. The fact the PIO said nothing of the functions of the CIP was more intriguing. He forwarded my application, perhaps thinking to safeguard the secret by taking me into it. I don't know. My one thought was - this beats the infantry.

Three weeks after Pearl Harbor, I was jerked out of a pre-OCS school and transferred into the secret CIP which became CIC [Counter Intelligence Corps} on 1 January 1942 — to confuse the enemy, no doubt. But the name change confused our army even more.

The secrecy was guarded so well, even from the army, that my service record for two years carried the innocuous statement that I was a sergeant at Fourth Service Command HQ. No mention was made of CIC on the record. Spies accessing these records would not uncover the secret that way!

In January 1942, I did not swelter in Georgia heat carrying rifle and pack. I was in Chicago in the first CIC training school and should have been content but somehow wasn't. I was now carrying a heavy weight - the secret. The weight went up as instructors repeated that not even relatives, best friends, Sunday school teacher or creditors must learn of CIC.

Former FBI, Secret Service and other super snoopers - tops in the country - taught all manner of tricks to guard the U.S. from enemy agents. A pleasant subject in the course was trailing a spy suspect [rabbit] around wintry Chicago streets in enjoyable temperatures 15 degrees below zero - and me from the south! There also were classes in judo, physical training and a daily stint on the school's roof clad only in shorts. And many other classes.

Most provoking was when we marched up and down city streets in civilian clothes so our officers could practice drilling. Grinning civilians yelled, "More draftees!" On the 10th day of this, I grinned back no more, I glared! My SP was setting in.

On completing school, I returned with my group to Atlanta to track spies with southern accents. Before being sent to my first assignment, it was again emphasized "Do not reveal the CIC or that you are even in the army. If asked, you're a civilian working for the War Department."

Some of us set up new district offices; some went to established ones. I was to open a new district. Most operated behind a smoke screen of "Such-and-such Insurance Company." I scorned these measures, as some curious noses could ask embarrassing questions.

I solved the problem of cover by examining FBI's setup. None of their offices were designated insurance, bakeries or toy factories; each had Federal Bureau of Investigation on the door. I noted known agents entered and departed, looking exactly like FBI agents - doing a good business, too.

So I broke with custom and left the space on my office door blank. No one ever opened it to ask about insurance, if they opened it they asked "What the hell do you do?"

Next step in developing SP came as friends and acquaintances wondered aloud when or if the army would get me. I wore glasses when passing army camps, to prevent GIs booing as they had been booed a week before. On furlough after 16 months service, my mother kept eyeing my civvies and worrying about my being out of uniform. I almost told her the truth but my secrecy oath was too strong. She must have believed she harbored an AWOL. She has yet to see me in uniform. That she takes my word I served in the army for 54 months is an outstanding example of mother-love.

After a few months under the secrecy demanded by HQ, unspoken thoughts of those around began to affect me. "Am I really in the army?" To test the reality of the situation, once I did not mail in the required daily report of activities. A warm, short and effective phone call from my colonel boss' office renewed my interest in reporting daily.

My respect for maintaining secrecy was jolted severely the day a munitions plant in my district phoned to report a "hot" sabotage case. Could I come out instantly to take charge of the investigation?

"That's why I'm here," I said - and did. That is, I got as far as the plant gate where an MP stopped me cold. There had been sabotage and he wasn't admitting anyone, as per orders.

"But look, here are my credentials to investigate that very case."

"They can be faked," he said.

I flashed my gold badge with "War Department, Military Intelligence" on it which we showed those who couldn't read. No go. After further arguments, a call to the Commanding General got me in. But you see what I mean about this secrecy stuff? I was learning its limitations. I soon discovered CIC agents overseas were able to do something about it.

"This is it" day finally came—CIC agents were needed abroad. Volunteer? Is that a joke, son? When I applied for CIP-CIC in peace time, we *all* volunteered for duty *anywhere*. As my only foreign language then was Spanish, overseas must mean Central or South America. Before I knew it, there I was in Australia, speaking passably good Australian.

In the Southwest Pacific Theater my SP began to disappear. HQ instructed us to acquaint the army and civilians around us of CIC's existence and mission. We gladly complied though it was a little late in the game to be fully satisfactory. For instance, during the battle for Manila while the struggle for the old walled section raged fiercely, I was blocks away at a "Veectoree" party, conscientiously advising a Filipino about CIC, how loyal Filipinos could help with evidence on spies and collaborators.

A young GI stood nearby with his mouth open at this revelation. After a few minutes he strode over, pushed me firmly and not gently into a seat whispering, "Listen, bud. If you are in intelligence, better stop spreading the news or I'll report you for loose talk, see?" He strolled away before I could ask how things were back home when he left.

No Filipino over six by war's end failed to know more about CIC than most Americans, as we had probably jailed at least one relative or acquaintance on collaboration or spying charges. We operated in the open with signs over offices reading "CIC" or "Counter Intelligence Corps." And even broadcast a CIC radio program! In that atmosphere of honest advertising, I thought my SP was cured.

When the war ended and I returned home, the first civilian I met asked, "What did you do in the army?"

"I was in the CIC," I answered proudly.

"Hell-o, what's that?" I had a relapse.

V

First Gabardine CIC School: Chicago 1942

IN CHICAGO JANUARY 1942 one month after Pearl Harbor, I was in a detachment of some 100-odd agents from U.S. Army Counter Intelligence Corps assigned to take an FBI course that, like much of my later military training, taught me very little I would ever use, in or out of the service. In Chicago we learned, among other things, how to pick locks, judo, lift fingerprints, make plaster molds of tire tracks, forge documents, and tail suspects. The last of activity, surveillance, was the centerpiece of our final exam and remains my most enduring memory of that wartime summer.

Although we were sergeants, our uniforms in Chicago were army-issue civilian, bought by voucher at government-approved outlets. We were therefore identically attired in tan gabardine suits, button-down white shirts, plain-toed brown shoes, and inconspicuous ties. Cold as it was, we had to wear jackets outdoors to conceal our mandatory shoulder holsters containing unloaded .38-caliber police-positive revolvers.

Our Chicago bivouac was a former YWCA building near the Water Tower on North Michigan Avenue. There were classrooms, cafeteria, gym, and double-decker bunks in the single rooms; being a U.S. Army installation, a "formation" was held early every morning on the roof top. Passers-by were naturally puzzled to see a platoon of apparently able-bodied young civilians in gabardine suits being put through close-order drill by a uniformed lieutenant. "Recruits" was his evasive reply to questioners, an explanation that grew less plausible as we marched around, week after week, in civilian disguise. At the time, the very existence of CIC was classified information.

As graduation day approached, we were told our final exam would be a "field exercise" in surveillance, which is the art of tracking someone's movements and activities while unobserved. For this purpose our class divided into equal groups of hares and hounds with each hare provided with a mimeographed sheet of instructions designed to give his assigned hound a hard time and perhaps shake him altogether. The hares were told when to take buses and taxis, where to get off, which shops to enter and what to buy, how far and direction to walk, what movie theatres and restaurants to enter {and how to depart}, and finally how to complete the exercise by registering at a designated hotel under an assumed German-sounding name. Our stalking activity was timed to last about two hours and take place entirely within the Loop.

The weather on exam day was cold and rainy. Older more sophisticated hounds arranged to meet discreetly with their hares in some warm tavern and there concoct plausible reports to give them both passing grades, reports in which hare would briefly elude his shadow and hound miss a few details (such as, brand of cigarette the suspect bought at the cafeteria). But both would get to the hotel lobby in time to check in and be observed doing so.

Most of us being fresh out of law practice undertook our assignments the conscientious and hard way. So we brought the war closer to home for Chicago cabbies as well as cops to whom we showed identification to explain headlong pursuit by taxi and on foot through tangled city traffic.

"God damn!" cried one excited cab driver as I flashed my shiny military intelligence badge and told him to trail my hare's vehicle. "The Nazi spies are sure out in force today. You're the fourth Secret Service agent I've picked up this afternoon, Lucky for us you boys are on the ball!" Off we went, through a red light on State Street where a cop waved us through at the sight of my badge.

On foot, we hounds stayed about 50 feet behind our subjects, on the opposite sidewalk, crossing at corners if they turned in one direction, pausing if they turned in the other, toward us. As instructed, both kept changing appearance by putting on and removing glasses, jackets, and hats. SOP in the spy world but not very effective in our case since now we knew our classmates' faces as well as our own. At any soda fountain where our hare might pause for coffee, we lingered at the far end of the counter until he paid before confronting the cashier with questions on what he had ordered and if he paid with coins or bills.

Curiously, no one seemed surprised or upset by our nosiness. One look at our credentials made everyone instantly eager to cooperate. In 1942, 1 guess it gave them a sense of participating in the war, if only vicariously.

Two hours is a long time on a January afternoon in Chicago; the hares slowed down and spent more time sitting in taxis and taking refreshment. Every step of the assignment had to be completed before we could head for the hotel where pseudo spies and saboteurs were to register as guests.

Arrangements had been made by the army so that various hotels would have a number of rooms available for this exercise, but there had been a slipup on our examination day. All hares had mistakenly received instructions to register at a single hotel—the Blackstone. So hares and hounds together converged almost simultaneously on the lobby, then filled with the traditional potted palms. Ten or so hounds crouched behind the plants while their assigned quarries besieged the reception desk, demanding registration forms they were to fill out with German names and addresses.

The paperwork completed, we hounds sprang out from behind the foliage, badges and credentials in hand, and ordered the clerks to show us forms and room assignments for all the Himmlers, Hindenburgs, Bismarcks, and Gorings who had checked in. Other occupants of the lobby only looked on with wide-eyed pride at seeing their boys in action against the enemies in our midst.

The course completed, we all dispersed-none of us, so far as I know, ever to wear our gabardines again. Within a month I was bound for Atlanta, where during the next two years was taught various other skills that I never again put to use. War's end found me on Luzon, where our U. S. summer seemed very long ago and faraway. By then I'd even forgotten how to pick a Jock. But it wasn't all a waste of time. Ask me even today to follow a suspicious stranger through city streets and I'll bet I can stay on his tail all the way home—provided he doesn't walk too fast.

VI

Air Force Fights for Its Own CIC

IN THE BEGINNING IT was the AC (Air Corps), a part of the U.S. Army. It had no investigative agency of its own like today's OSI. Until 1 January 1942, it borrowed agents from the Army G2's CIP (Corps of Intelligent Police) to check on suspicious plane and other incidents associated with the AC.

On 1 January 1942, the CIP was renamed the CIC (Counter Intelligence Corps) with the same agents but a new name. The Army Corps Area (later renamed Service Commands) G2s continued lending these agents to the AC as before. The nearby agent usually assigned on the case made his report to his own G2 who passed the results on to the AC. Under the 1939 Delimitation's Agreement between FBI, ONI [Office of Naval Intelligence] and the Army this arrangement continued a few months into 1942.

With WW2 on, there was an increase in suspicious incidents. The AC clamored for more agents, actually desiring to control and train them to handle its own special problems and operations.

First Step Towards This Goal

Not too soon, a start began 27 April 1942 with 154 officers and 39:4 agents authorized for 12 AF and 94 ferrying stations. By January 1943, that quota was still unfilled. CIC never had enough agents for both Army and AC, the AC (now Air Force), which had been promised 25% of CIC's total. By informal agreement with the 4th Service Command G2, the AF set up its own first CIC detachment at Southeast AF Training Center.

On 4th and 5th May 1943, CIC agreed to continue to supply agents to AF, with control and supervision by the latter but kept the power to recall and reassign its agents through the Service Commands if needed. The AF in turn could call on local CIC detachments for more help in an emergency. The total assigned or scheduled for the AF on 22 July 1943 was 34 officers, 195 agents - while estimated needs were for 344 officers and 963 agents.

Next Step: Special Air Force Training

AAF [Army AF] had its close ties cut with the Army beginning November, 1943. All CIC agents with it now came under the general supervision of the Chief, CIC, AAF, with immediate supervision under A2s. But requests for off base assistance continued from A2s to local CIC units. All agents with AAF had gone through CIC training schools, but AAF required them also to possess the abilities and training to detect saboteurs, etc., at aircraft depots and installations.

Special schools for AAF CIC followed at PA State School *of* Aeronautics, Middletown Air Service Command, and Chanute Field IL. An Aircraft Mechanics course was at Hill Field, Ogden UT for those without prior mechanical training.

Jurisdiction Clarified

The Army Adjutant General clarified by letter 24 May 1944 that the AAF was to maintain self-sufficient CI networks, with its own CIC held responsible for investigating sabotage, espionage, subversion and disaffection of AAF personnel; loyalty checks of AAF military personnel; security surveys and investigations of AAF materiel and installations; violations of military information security within AAF; undeveloped leads outside AAF channels by coordination through the local SC (Army Service Command), and strict observance of MIS jurisdiction under the current Delimitation's Agreement, furnish local SC with reports of its investigations and establish its own liaison direct with the FBI and ONI.

AAF prohibited its CIC agents from POW interrogations, combat intelligence missions, black market, moral turpitude and criminal investigations—and KP, fatigue or general guard duty.

Many cases arose out of incidents involving aircraft or materiel where there was a possibility or indication of sabotage. All these were the result of intent or negligence. If the first, investigation was to determine the guilty party; if negligence, to find out if it was intentional or accidental and the person responsible. Most often it was not sabotage - but non-sabotage reports were still valuable to prevent future accidents and losses, ultimately leading to revised technical manuals, modified designs, corrected production methods, and new or upgraded safety programs.

Activation of AAF CIC Units

The integrated AAF intelligence service had finally begun. All agents now with AAF were transferred to AAF HQ Sqdn, Bolling Field, Washington DC. Recognizing the difficulties CIC agents faced, the AAF ordered no CIC officer or agent was to be assigned to fatigue or administrative duties except as required by its own detachment. In turn, CIC officers had jurisdiction only over their teams, with no command authority over non-CIC sections of squadrons.

June 21, 1944, activation of CIC units under AAF resulted in a total of 231 officers, 592 agents [TO&E 30500] for detachments with 12 major commands. Sub-detachments went to bases and important installations in their respective areas. With agents now on duty providing CI coverage at more than 235 AAF installations, on 24 July 1944 the major units were designated with numbers from 601 to 604, and 700 to 707. The AAF HQ unit became number 700. HQ for Air Force Transportation Corps was 707; for all agents with Air Force within Continental U.S. it was 706. Wherever the AAF had a base or station anywhere in the world, it now had a nearby CIC agent on call.

August 1944, AAF began procuring and training additional agents when the Army CIC schools were abolished [See *America's Secret Army* and *Spy Catchers of the U.S. Army in the War with Japan*] leaving the AAF, Manhattan Project (Atom Bomb) and Transportation Corps [seaport ship paneling units] CIC agents untouched. The Chief , CIC, AAF now issued badges and credentials for its new agents, while retaining the high standards demanded by the War Department for CIC agents in the whole Army structure. SC assistance and cooperation was appreciated.

In 1947, AAF cut loose more completely from Army to become USAAF. Its CIC was combined with Air Police to become today's OSI, Office of Special Investigations - same mission with criminal investigations added. With detachments wherever needed around the world, an OSI agent may be eligible for membership in National CIC Association!

VII

Manhattan Project: Special Agent Gleaves

We've seen too few articles about agents assigned to protect our Manhattan Project – the Atom Bomb. It's ironic this one comes from an obituary. But it shows the importance of our members sending in obits and stories of agents when seen in print.

RAYMOND LESLIE "LES" GLEAVES spent World War II in civilian clothes in San Francisco as an Army counter intelligence officer assigned to the Manhattan Project, which developed the atomic bomb ending WW2.

Gleaves was assigned to the Army's Counter Intelligence Corps and stationed in Arkansas before becoming part of a 10-man team in San Francisco, where his mission was to protect the atomic secret. CIC agent Gleaves' intelligence work mostly involved following people who were considered potential threats to the atomic project around California or listening in on taps to their telephones, he said in a 14-page story of his life prepared for his family in 1997.

He once interviewed a man on the pretense of checking out an associate.

"I was 'casing the joint' so our telephone boys could install a mike in the light over a small eating table," he wrote decades later.

Another time, he was a courier flying from San Francisco to Oak Ridge TN with a top-secret packet strapped to his back.

While World War II espionage was a significant part of his father's life, the hard times of the Great Depression probably had a bigger impact on Mr. Gleaves, said his son, Jim Gleaves of Houston.

"The experience he had during the Depression made him financially conservative, very frugal and very, very careful," his son said. "He wanted stability for his family. He was always a very meticulous man, and I think that was instrumental in him being selected for the Counter Intelligence Corps."

Born near Van Alstyne, Texas, Gleaves grew up in Plainview and Weslaco TX , and Fort Lauderdale FL before graduating from North Dallas High School in 1930. A hurricane sent the family back to Texas.

He went to Rice Institute [now University] but could not afford living expenses, even though tuition was then free. He spent $600 in savings his first year at Rice.

He returned to Rice's Houston campus in September 1932, but "jobs were too scarce, and they were saved for desperate men with families," he said in 1997.

Spring 1933 he worked for several months on Ford Motor Co.'s assembly line in East Dallas, where he had 90 seconds to install a fuel tank on each of 40 cars passing his station each hour for a pay of $5 a day. Tiring of conditions in the assembly plant he returned to his dad's produce business before enrolling in night law school. Gleaves worked his way through law school, passing the state bar two months before receiving his law degree from Southern Methodist University.

After the war, Gleaves returned to North Texas, where he had a long career with Veterans Administration before buying and operating Oak Cliff Personnel Service. Gleaves, 93, died June 17 of natural causes at the Gardens of Richardson nursing home. He had lived in Richardson since 1953 and had a stroke three years ago. He was a long time member of First United Methodist Church of Richardson. Services were Wednesday in Dallas. He was buried in Restland Memorial Park. His wife, Ethel T. Gleaves, died in December. In addition to his son, Gleaves is survived by a daughter, Gail G. Booth of Anna, Texas, and four grandchildren.

VIII

The Afro-American Army and Race Riots

DID YOU KNOW THAT early in World War II there was a race riot in Louisiana involving thousands of soldiers and civilians? And at the height of World War II, an Afro-American Army was forming in the deep south of our nation with the aim of taking over certain states and sever them from the United States into a separate nation for the black races in America?

Lee Street Riot

Well, son, it's the truth. The race riot termed the Lee Street Riot took place in Alexandria, Louisiana. There were similar disturbances in other states, though the first one was in Louisiana.

Black CIC agent Thornton R. Greene, an Alabama native, made his mark in connection with the investigation of black soldiers rioting in Alexandria LA. It started when a white MP arrested a black soldier for creating a disturbance on Lee Street about 8 P. M., Saturday January 10th 1942.

When the black soldier began resisting arrest, onlookers became angry and physical—resulting in the Lee Street Riot. Nearby black soldiers joined in, as did other white as well as black Military Police. Additional military police were quickly called in from Camp Livingston, along with city and state police.

At the height of the action some 60 MPs, 30 city police and state troopers, and an undetermined number of white civilians engaged an estimated "several thousand black troops along a four or five block corridor of Lee Street, also called Little Harlem." Guns were fired, tear gas bombs were thrown, with the blacks hurling bricks, rocks, and sticks. In the melee some 28 black soldiers were injured, at least three of them seriously. One or more policemen were injured; one black civilian was shot in the hip. Many black civilians were trapped in the two-hour turmoil before authorities brought order out of chaos.

Rumors went wild about the two-hour race riot; exaggerated reports stated that 18 had been killed and as many as 26 wounded. The main concern of Army Military Intelligence was whether the incident was the work of subversive elements or enemy provocateurs.

CIC special agent Thornton R. Greene was immediately dispatched to Alexandria to check on this possibility. Greene's findings cleared early fears that the riot was enemy inspired; his report concluded "the underlying cause of the disturbances and controversy in Alexandria is not due to any subversive element, but ... to jealousy, hate, roughness, and over-indulgence in intoxicants."

Greene was in great demand, not only in our Service Command, but also by others such as the FBI, which had no black agents at that time. The investigation into the race riot on Lee Street [more or less the border between black and white] was for all intents and purposes practically over when white CIC Special Agent Duval A Edwards, who was in the Chicago CIC School in January 1942, got there the first week in February.

Greene had been sent to cover the black part of town and the black troops in the nearby four army camps and one air corps field; Edwards followed up on leads among the white troops that had not been completed by Special Agent Charles Bruder being replaced by Edwards. Greene's findings cleared early fears that the riot was enemy inspired.

As the case involved both U. S. Army blacks and civilians not employed by the army, it was obviously a case of joint jurisdiction with the FBI. We have no copy of the FBI's report. With only one FBI agent in that area, he probably left most of the work to CIC.

The Afro-American Army

This case was entirely within the jurisdiction of CIC. While our troops were overseas fighting the Nazis in Europe and the Japanese in the Pacific, the CIC faced serious trouble from blacks in the Fourth Service Command, headquartered in Atlanta. Many of our army training camps were scattered throughout this command, so when an ambitious young black soldier we'll call "Willy Jones" started his own secret army that he named the "Afro-American Army," our Military Intelligence was rightly concerned.

The Afro-American Army proposed a black nation to be formed out of the states of Georgia, North and South Carolina, Florida, and Alabama. News spread quickly around the many black units training in the south.

Promoter Jones named himself "General" and began recruiting officers for his army by asking for a monetary compensation for each class of officer. For example: a recruit might become a Second Lieutenant for $100, a First Lt. for $200, Captain for $400, Major for $1000, Lieutenant Colonel for $1,500, a full Colonel for $2,000.

Word of the Afro-American Army reached CIC Headquarters in Atlanta while it was still on paper. M. I. promptly classified it a threat. At the very least it fell into the category of disaffection, and certainly was subversive activity within wartime CIC's mission. Real disaffection hurt the Army in a number of ways that could lead to outright disloyalty, harmful to the training of soldiers in any service command.

Black CIC agents Thornton R. Greene and George Kennedy were assigned to penetrate this newly reported Afro-American "army" and secure evidence needed to end its existence. They each separately contacted the "General" with ease, paying the asking fee for officer's ranks that certainly far exceeded their enlisted grades.

Their purchased ranks were high enough to enable each to sit in on General Jones planning staff. When they had accumulated enough hard evidence on the extent of the secret army's operation, the data was turned over to prosecutors.

Ringleader General Jones was arrested before he had progressed beyond a paper army. Put on trial, he was convicted and sentenced to a number of years in prison beyond the end of WW2.

Years later, agent Greene expressed his opinion to the writer that the black general was in a number of ways sincere in his opinion that black Americans were entitled to a portion of the deep south states for themselves, and his openness in court on this point was sufficient to ensure his conviction. But of course his activity was an impediment to our war efforts, and had to be stopped — which CIC-SIC agents Greene and Kennedy neatly did.

What was not mentioned was the obvious problems northern blacks training in the south faced under the time-engrained Jim Crow practiced throughout the southern states, which the Army failed to consider. A northern black could not see why he had to go the back of a bus on a ticket that cost the same as a white. Nor drink from a fountain marked "For blacks only;" or go to the back door of most cafes and restaurants for food that cost him the same as white customers.

IX

Biak Jungle Tales

AT SUPPER THAT EVENING, Duval sat with other members of the headquarters company. He didn't know them by their names, as he had been with the unit less than a week, working almost exclusively with Miyamoto, and occasionally with the I&R platoon Captain and his men.

A corporal named John was talking as Duval seated himself as comfortably as possible, but in a position to fight the battle with the flies. Luckily, it was not as hot as daylight was beginning to fade and the pests were not so prevalent. All present knew however that with nightfall the other flying enemy, the mosquito, would take the field. The best defense there was to be inside a jungle hammock, even though it could not be efficiently strung inside a foxhole. It still afforded some protection from biting insects.

The conversation during the meal turned, as it inevitably seemed to with GIs, to home, or some aspect of it. John was saying, "I was born in a saddle, on a horse my Mom was riding across the prairies of central Texas."

Laughter.

"That's an oldie, John," and "I think I can beat that. I was born on third base, while my Mom was waiting for a fly ball with one out, to get her home. She never made it, but I did - that's where I got my nickname 't.b.' — which stands for third base. I never could hit a home run, but got lots of three baggers."

Each of the half dozen in the group tried to outdo the rest, and the group fell silent as it became Duval's turn. He was an outsider, a newcomer. Curiosity was plain to see on every face turned to him expectantly.

"Well," he started, "Can't say as I have anything startling to tell about my birth. Certainly not as exciting as my Mother being in a softball game just as I was being born."

"Tarnation," Texan John exclaimed, "I figure, with your accent yore bound to be from Louisiana, or Mississippi or ..."

"You're right," Duval said. "But I sorta hate to talk about my birthplace, coz most people laugh, and it wasn't a laughing matter - to me, or my folks."

"Come on," T.D. cajoled. "We got lotsa time. Of course we'll believe you. Won't we guys. Why shouldn't we?"

"Weeel, all right," Duval seemed to relent. "Maybe, if I can give yawl a little background first. You see, back before World War 1 - and you won't find this in the history books, for reasons that will be plain enough to see - a German submarine was discovered coming up the Mississippi. We weren't in the war then, but I guess that Germans figured we would be getting into it, and were doing some earlier reconnoitering - maybe planting a spy in New Orleans."

Every face was turned intently in Duval's direction. This was new material, and different from the usual banter and jocularity.

"It was the Louisiana National guard that discovered the submarine, actually in an evening much like this. The sub captain had come up to the surface in a tributary of the Mississippi, back in the swamps. But it just so happened that the Louisiana

Guard had a training camp, on the banks of this slough. Well, the Guard caught the sub and all the men on it unawares, and took them prisoners. Even though we weren't in the war, they knew there was no good reason for the sub to be where they found it. And sure enough the sub captain could not and did not offer any. He and his crew were put under guard at the camp; the commander of the Guard contacted headquarters which sent a message to the White House, to President Wilson."

"Well, President Wilson was a smart cookie. He knew the U.S. was not prepared to go to war at that moment over this incident, so he ordered the Louisiana National Guard to cool it, in fact, to conceal the incident completely, by hiding the sub and keeping the crew in the swamps away from everybody and especially the press."

"The upshot of the whole thing was that one of the guard, in fact the one who had first spotted the sub, knew a little bit about running one of them. So the decision was made to put a small crew on the sub, take it further back into the swamps, submerge it far enough so that only the conning tower was above the water, camouflage the tower to look like a duck blind - and thus conceal it until we entered the war. This gave our country time to prepare for the inevitable."

"Well, it was done that way. Except, not knowing how long it would take, the three crewmen were allowed to bring their families and live on the submarine. The crew were dressed as hunters, the families remained below, being entertained by reading material."

"Well, as yawl have probly guessed by now, my Mom was pregnant, and sure enough, I figure now that she was actually about ten feet below the surface of the Ouchita river when I first say the light of day. Yep, I was born on a German sub, originally named the Nautilus by the way, some ten feet plus under water."

Silence. Texas John stirred. "Why haven't we heard about any of this in some history book, somewhere, hunh?"

"Well, that's easy," explained Duval, "the German crew, for one thing, tried to break out of prison, and every one of them died, either from gunfire, drowning in the swamps or from being bitten by cotton mouths - cotton mouths, that's water moccasins, yawl."

"And," he forestalled other doubters, "all of the Louisiana National Guards went into the U.S. Army the day after we declared war on the Germans. They had been sworn to secrecy about this submarine bit. And every one of them was killed in the first engagement against the enemy in France."

"And," he went on, "if anybody ever checked the records at the State headquarters, they must have doubted the story, because they had nobody to check the facts with. You see, the three crewmen on the submarine had taken it so far into the swamps and backwoods, that the rest of the Guard didn't actually know where it was. So nobody on board knew we had gone to war until months had passed. They took the sub back down river, and found a deserted guard camp at the old site. But they also found copies of newspapers that revealed we had gone to war with Germany and all the Louisiana National Guard unit supposedly had been shipped out."

"Well, what would you do?" Duval asked with a quaver in his voice, "the guard crew on the sub were not professional soldiers. And they all had their families with them. They made a decision right then and there that they would take the sub back up the Ouchita, eek out a living hunting and trapping, and leave the shooting war to others."

The silence deepened, if silence can deepen.

"And if any of yawl still have some doubts," Duval stated firmly, "you should know that I am a champion underwater swimmer. I've been swimming under water all my life. It's known as early conditioning, you know. I had only been born a few months when my Dad stuck me in that torpedo tube, pulled the trigger and shot me out of the Nautilus like I was a torpedo."

X

Harry L. Amerman, CIC Agent of 201st with 1st Armored Corps in Italy

Amerman died in 1948 in Vienna, Austria. His story came from a niece rewritten by Duval A. Edwards

Harry L. Amerman's Story

LANDING AT SALERNO, ITALY 11 Sept. 1943, CIC Special Agent Amerman was placed in charge of CIC at the advance Command Post, Fifth Army, then located on the banks of Sele River. His mission: to establish contact with refugees and disbanded Italian soldiers for the purpose of recruiting and dispatching agents behind the lines to pinpoint enemy locations.

The combat situation was fluid, with little information on German dispositions around the beachhead perimeter. Under constant enemy fire, Amerman led his CIC agents into the forward areas around Altavilla village and surrounding territory. Several towns in the region, such as Montecello, Olevano and Selito, were not yet occupied by Allied troops. He set up CIC HQ in Olevano, from where a network of informants was built up extending through the front lines.

German Soldiers in Civvies

Tracing rumors of isolated German units, Amerman organized and led a searching party that combed caves and hills, capturing German soldiers who had changed into civvies and mingled with the refugees. Interrogation of these prisoners coupled with information from the informant network enabled Amerman to provide Fifth Army G-2 with extensive combat intelligence — including locations of depots, materiel, mined areas, artillery positions — and extensive information on the German Order of Battle. All of this was extremely valuable at the time because of the changing tactical situation and scarcity of knowledge of German strength and dispositions.

Following the success of his initial mission, Amerman was placed in charge of the security detail at Fifth Army CP during the Italian campaign. Security was accomplished by diligent checks before sites were selected and occupied, then by constant inspection, advice and planning during their occupation. These measures contributed largely to the safety and security of all headquarters troops from possible espionage or sabotage.

This mission was performed at these sites: Naples, Caserta, Fresanzano, Sparanise and Anzio.

Anzio Breakout and Drive

Shortly before the Allied breakout at the Anzio beachhead, Amerman was put in charge of its security program. Here the focus was on preventing possible leaks of information on the forthcoming breakout and following drive.

During the final advance on Rome, he was placed in charge of a CIC detachment in the former Fascist political center of Littoria. From there, he organized skillfully and with extreme competence the security operations of CIC teams deployed from the banks of the Garigliano River to the forward lines.

Bronze Star Award

It comes as no surprise that Agent Amerman was proposed for an award. And it was done by his commanding officer who had followed his exploits "during the period mentioned and [had] personal knowledge of the service" Amerman had performed.

At the time of service, the agent was a 2d Lt., M.I., CIC, Fifth Army. In August 1944 Harry L. Amerman was awarded the Bronze Star for the foregoing cited actions. When presented the award, he was a 1st Lt, MI, CO of 6794th CIC Detachment (Ovhd), HQ, Fifth Army.

All of the foregoing information has been extracted from the Recommendation for Award by the Chief, 305th CIC, 5th Army dated 18 August 1944. That Chief, as many know, was NCICA's own Stephen J. Spingam!

XI

Santa Rosa, Laguna de Bay

As fighting for Manila's Walled City went on in February and March, 1945, our agents had no chance to meet Filipinos outside of our mission. As senior agent, I managed the 214th CIC office tracking our agents covering Manila and Cavite. After six weeks, I asked our CO to assign me to outside cases.

The 11th CIC [11th Air Borne Division] was on the move, leaving cases unfinished and prisoners awaiting incarceration in Santa Rosa, Laguna de Bay, near Manila. Time for relief by the 214th CIC, so the CO sent me to this office, with two special agents assisting me.

The 11th CIC had occupied the best home in Santa Rosa, previously housing Japan's secret police, the *Kempei Tai*. Local guerrillas [cleared by the 11th CIC] greeted my team, assuring a 24-hour guard around the dwelling in the absence of U.S. troops in town. After months in foxholes and hammocks, we were in Hog Heaven[!]: The two-storied house possessed that marvelous bathroom commode, and a bath tub!

Water didn't come from the tap but this was easily solved. When we were in New Guinea natives had no money system, Luzon was different. CIC agents had confidential fund authority. Seeing how the 11th CIC lived and worked, I realized what confidential funds could do.

With the guerrillas' help, I hired a staff of civilians. The first: a young lad to fill the upstairs bath tub and commode with water, clean the house, and wield a huge fan to keep flies at bay during meals; an assistant for a cook left behind by the 11th, to make K-rations palatable with fresh fish, eggs (duck) and meat; a laundry lady was lined up; and finally a majordomo to oversee this staff.

A large room upstairs was ideal for interviews and report writing. Guerrillas and citizens nearby came to reveal traitors and collaborators. To speed up taking statements, I hired a secretary [all male] for each agent and myself. Our guards halted everyone at the entrance, bringing us the name and business of each caller. Thanks to the marvelous support, loyalty and cooperation of the people of Santa Rosa, CIC was in business. A report of the cases and pertinent data went daily to my CO at 214th. Knowing he would drop in one day, I wondered if he would approve.

Unfinished 11th CIC cases kept us busy. Daily our guards announced informants from as far away as Cavite. My senior agent, Charlie Michod, suggested that as many guerrillas called themselves majors and up, the team should match them in rank to keep them coming. If they knew we were enlisted special agents, they might demand to see only officers. To keep informants talking, I took the highest rank I had yet, colonel; Michod became a major, Keaton, a captain.

Anyone of Japanese descent automatically came on our suspect list, until cleared. This included mestizos of half-Japanese blood. One case I investigated personally was a mestiza living in a Santa Rosa barrio, married to a Filipino. She was home with her children in a typical bamboo house in a barrio. In her thirties, she had distinctive Japanese features, not always a definite test. She talked frankly after my halting Tagalog put her at ease. After a half-hour, she offered liquid refreshment that I politely refused. I decided she was not a security risk, and was needed at home to care for the children. Guerrillas who knew everybody in the barrios later confirmed this. Her husband might have been a Makapili or Ganap guerrilla; but that did not warrant a mother being imprisoned for her bloodline.

One day a guard ran upstairs to report Japanese soldiers nearby in broad daylight, the guerrillas needed help as they possessed only a few ancient guns. CIC agents were armed; I carried a tommy gun with several clips, in addition to my shoulder-holster .38 Colt. Only two enemy were reported, but others could be near. Quickly considering the situation, I decided to help alone for several reasons: my weapon had greater fire power, I had more basic infantry training, and was not married as my agents were. I did not want to endanger them as this was not ostensibly within CIC's spy-catching mission. Following the guerrillas to the enemy's reported hiding place, I wondered if they were stragglers, or were trying to reach contacts in Santa Rosa. For instance, the mestiza I had interviewed a few days earlier?

I never got an answer. Nearing the target, suddenly "bees buzzed" by my head. Bullets! Now leading the patrol, falling to the ground automatically I fired a burst from the tommy gun -- and heard guerrillas shout! I had hit both soldiers, killing one instantly; the other was dispatched by a guerrilla. Regretting we did not capture and question them, their ages were placed under 21.

Walking back to the office I dreaded what my CO would say. I didn't have to wait, he was visiting; spotting me and the dead Japanese carried by the guerrillas, he jumped on me for risking my life on a non-CIC mission. Had there been evidence of an effort to contact a Ganap or Makapili, it would have made a difference.

Local people warmed up to this tiny American unit occupying the best *malaking tahanan* — mansion — in town. The mayor dropped by to say it was victory celebration time — and we occupied the expected location for the party. The mayor invited key people and provided some food, we supplied some food and refreshments. We filled four empty Four Roses bottles with *tuba* or *lumbanog*, a strong coconut brew, and shared canned Spam, a rare treat for the Filipinos.

Our most reliable informant, provincial *piskal* [judge] Juan Pambuan, wrote a speech I delivered in Tagalog. [After WW2, he was governor of the province of Santa Rosa]. We sang native folk-songs [*kondimun*] and Spanish songs with Tagalog words: including *Táyuna sa Antipolo* [Let's All Go to Antipolo], and *Palomang Mahal* [The Dove]. Folks enjoyed the toasting and drinking. The mayor and I tried to out-toast each other. Result: the second time in my life I ended up tipsy. At least I was "home" and had only to ascend the stairs to fall in bed – far better than on that 1944 Christmas day on an Admiralty island, when I got drunk the first time ever, and on 3.2 beer – and crawled back to the dock to board a boat to my ship, the *U.S. Mount Olympus*!

Santa Rosa was such a friendly town, I felt at home the few weeks I was there. I could not stay when, a surprised CIC agent, I was granted a field commission and under the rules had to be transferred to another unit. Still believing no legal army order could be refused, I accepted even though most enlisted soldiers believed a Master Sergeant was higher than a 2nd lieutenant any time.

But I had been specially requested by the CIC detachment at Sixth Army HQ, so found my way there after one night at XIVth Corps HQ on duty as Officer of the Day. Arriving at Sixth Army I was greeted by other new 2nd lieutenants: Mike Horwitz, Baltimore attorney; Bill Owens, PhD, professor from Texas A&M. Jim English, writer and former editor on Boy's Life magazine. We had come to Brisbane, Australia MacArthur's theater in the same shipment of 12 agents, then assigned to separate missions.

Mike was serving as the 214th Executive Officer, Jim as personnel director of the unit, and all units under our jurisdiction, Bill Owens was leaving days for home after winning a Legion of Merit medal for recruiting a regiment of Hukbahaps into Philippine Scouts, serving a much needed function guarding strategic bridges and points on the supply line to front line troops. The job awaiting me was investigation officer, supervising all CIC investigations within Sixth Army's jurisdiction.

Both Mike and Bill were ten years older than I; I glowed in their friendships. We continued a close friendship long after the war until their demise.

XII

Manhattan District CIC's *Astounding* Case

CIC's most hush-hush detachment in WW2 was the one guarding the top-secret atom bomb project, The Manhattan District. CIC agents assigned to that detachment have observed their oath not to discuss what they did, even with their fellow agents. Thanks to the Ann Bray history and declassification of most operations, and to having more time available, I bring an unusual case to the attention of other CIC veterans.

"WHERE DID YOU GET *this* idea?" demanded CIC agent Arthur E. Rielly, confronting the editor of a pulp science fiction magazine in NY City in 1944.

"I take full responsibility for the technical part of the story," the editor replied calmly. "Author Steve Cartmill supplied the plot, but based it on my technical background, including my work in physics at MIT."

The agent was there because of a story by Cartmill titled "Deadline" published in the magazine's March 1944 issue. Safeguarding the top secret Atom Bomb project, Army CIC was heavily involved in protecting any and all information that hinted even vaguely of uranium or atomic energy, or the nature of the work of Manhattan District that would shorten the war.

Cartmill's story was laid on an alien earth-like planet and told of a commando successfully destroying an atom bomb held by a Nazi-like power planned for use against the hero's homeland. The magazine's international readership included neutral Sweden, a hot bed of espionage. There was danger the story might reach the enemy and provide its intelligence with an idea of our progress in perfecting a super bomb.

Director of Censorship Byron Price had issued a confidential letter on 28 June 1943 to all editors and broadcasters requesting they avoid any mention of atomic energy or any of the various elements with which the Project was experimenting.

Had this science-fiction magazine overlooked this request? Watchful eyes set up to report violations saw enough in "Deadline" to alarm Manhattan's Security of a possible leak that could reach enemy eyes.

CIC agents went on the move at once. Team leader Rielly found the magazine's editor-in-chief' in, showed him War Department credentials, source of the story and its background along with all information pertaining to it and anyone involved, including the editor.

The Big Apple phase of the investigation had only begun. An informant editor had lunched with Edgar R. Norton, engineer with a classified Bell Laboratories unit not connected with Manhattan Project. Had Norton spilled knowledge to the editor from friends with Manhattan District's Murray Hill New Jersey project?

Agent Rielly questioned Norton closely.

"Utterly fantastic," Norton exclaimed. "Of course I know about the story. I reviewed it for the magazine before it was published, and reported I thought it was a childish attempt. Its technical part was common knowledge. Any classified information in it was pure coincidence."

An additional person at the luncheon was science-fiction writer Will Jenkins whose pen name was Murray Leinster. He told Rielly he and his daughter Mary "had conducted experiments on acquiring quantities of atomic copper." The results were sent to scientist/writer Isaac Asimov at Columbia University to analyze. But the mass spectrograph there broke, so there was no analysis. Denied security clearance, Jenkins had resigned from the Office of War Information.

The trail led next from Asimov to writers associated with the same science-fiction magazine: Robert Heinlein, and Sprague de Camp. Heinlein admitted he was a friend of Cartmill, and corresponded with him on matters nuclear.

B. W. Menke in the District Security Division set in motion the investigation of author Steve Cartmill, then living in Manhattan Beach CA. This part of the investigation was under the direction of R. S. Killough of the Manhattan District's Berkeley office, and lasted through April 1944.

A mail cover was begun March 11 on Cartmill and his family. Files of FBI, MI and local police were checked, as well as those of ONI. The latter revealed before the war Cartmill's father had tried to interest the Japanese Consulate in NY in a machine gun design after it was turned down by the American War Department. CIC found no involvement in this by Cartmill.

With the help of the Manhattan Beach Postmaster and before he interviewed Cartmill, Killough engaged Stewart Hoffman, mail carrier on the route, to have an oblique conversation about the story with Cleve. Hoffman, a sci-fi fan, had read Deadline; as he read the story, he thought it might be investigated.

Hoffman reported back to Killough that Cartmill's reaction to Deadline was that "it stinks," and wanted to talk more about a story he had written and sold to *Collier's*. Hoffman believed the science-fiction story was entirely from Cartmill's own imagination.

Killough then interviewed Cartmill under pretext, revealing neither his identity nor mission. Cleve stated his story was first laid on Earth, but changed to off-planet on advice of the editor "to avoid any conflict with wartime censorship." Killough stated in his report that "Cleve is educated enough to be able to piece out the facts on which to base such a story from his own reading from pre-war publications readily available."

When this report reached Rielly, the contradiction with the editor's statement about the technical portion was enough to throw the case into higher gear. An open interview with Cartmill was decided on.

On 3 May 1944, Special Agent D. L. Johnson, also from the Project's Berkeley office, went to Cartmill and asked point-blank about Deadline. This interview provided the only solid answers they were able to get, but failed to reveal if there was a leak at Manhattan Project. That was never established.

Cartmill denied having prophetic powers, but it turned out he had more technical background than his editor had credited him with. Though not a scientist, he had worked for the American Radium Products Company in Los Angeles, and studied radium and its properties there. After he left the firm, he continued these studies. He had branched out into uranium, discussing U-235 and atomic energy with science-fiction writers and scientists Robert Heinlein, Jack Williamson and others. He knew de Camp, Asimov, and Jenkins by reputation.

He had *never* met the magazine editor but admitted that for the technical material he took the major part from letters sent him by the editor, plus a minor part from his own knowledge. He showed the agent all correspondence with the editor, which on reading Johnson became convinced Cartmill was telling the truth. Questioning the author about telling the mail carrier the technical aspects were his own, the author confessed he could not allow a science-fiction fan to think that all the data in Deadline did not originate with the author; he thought this was a writer's prerogative.

A three-page letter from the editor, dated 16 August 1943, revealed the editor knew U-235 had been separated into quantities permitting further research. That letter provided not only enough technical know-how but even the plot that Cartmill expanded on, including taking place on another planet.

By now, the agents had gotten a quick education on science-fiction writing, though they failed to spot earlier published stories on nuclear weapons and atomic energy. They felt the situation did not warrant further investigation into a possible leak.

Not so at Oak Ridge HQ whose LTC Parsons wrote a bitter memo to LTC John Lansdale, Security chief in Washington, stating that even if the publication of Deadline did not violate the censorship code, it could provoke public speculation and thus endanger the Project's security efforts. He even suggested having the postal service revoke the mailing privileges of all such publications! This was never acted upon, but resulted in a reminder from the Officer of Censorship to Street and Smith, magazine publishers, of the danger to our security of such stories. Censorship did write to the editor in question to tone down on any further subjects "involved in our request of June 28, 1943."

But when made aware of the story's possible consequences in the hands of the enemy, the editor readily *volunteered* to do so. In his initial interview, he had already stated he would suppress the Deadline issue from subscribers and distribution in Sweden.

CIC could now close the case with the simple title *"Astounding."*

The editor however was to relate the story of CIC's visit to his office to many friends until his death!

As some readers may have guessed, the pulp magazine that brought this case about was *Astounding Science-Fiction* edited by John W. Campbell, Jr., from 1937 [it began in 1930]. He continued in this role throughout WW2 until his death. Along with editor Hugo Gernsback of the pioneer science fiction magazine *Amazing Stories*, he became a legend to science-fiction writers and readers for his scientific knowledge.

Astounding now is published with the intriguing title of *Analog Science Fiction and Fact* under the capable leadership of editor Stanley Schmidt, also a science-fiction writer, who still maintains its high standards as "hard science-fiction." Every issue has a fact article about the latest developments in space, as well as other scientific areas and theories. These are by writers and scientists who know their subjects and write with clarity for ordinary readers to understand.

The fiction making up the bulk of the magazine has to contain known scientific facts to be published, which makes it "hard science-fiction," as opposed to others now crowding this now popular field, many falling into the "bug-eyed monster" fantasy category.

XIII

CIC in Alaska

For several years before WWII, Alaska was recognized as needing careful counterintelligence coverage. Since trained investigative personnel were not available, an extensive military and civilian informant system supervised by Col. Lawrence Castner, S-2, served as a substitute. In July 1941 CIP agents Thomas Chambers and Charles Dowling arrived to investigate questionable individuals and organizations. When CIP became CIC, seven more agents joined them from HQ, Western Defense Command and FOURTH Army; by May 1943 this number had grown to twelve, four of them officers. On 1 November 1943 the Alaskan Defense Command was renamed the Alaska Department, and designated a separate Theater of Operations. Nearly as large as all of western Europe, Alaska's vast territory required setting up several field offices in addition to the CIC HQ at Fort Richardson: Fairbanks, Juneau, Ketchikan, Anchorage, Adak and Shemya.

DURING A 1943 INSPECTION trip of Alaska, Lowell Bradford (out of CIC HQ at the War Department in D.C.) painfully was made aware that frequent trips were necessary between CIC HQ at Fort Richardson and the Fairbanks field office 270 miles away; the inclement weather, absence of a rail and road net- work, and the slowness of water travel made these trips hazardous indeed. There is no record of any change in the setup caused by the inspection; it is just another example of CIC doing its job as well as it could under very trying circumstances.

As late as 1945 CIC depended on dog teams and sleds for access even to the relatively populous sectors of the territory. Weather was a constant, serious problem; while large parts of Alaska, especially in the southeast, enjoyed relatively mild weather in winter and summer, northern Alaskan temperatures often were lower than 60 degrees BELOW zero.

In the early days of WWII, CIC operations in Alaska were carried on by agents working solely in an undercover capacity, taking jobs as civilians or pretending to be employees at various government agencies. They carefully concealed any connection with military intelligence, except in their dealings with the many contacts in the extensive information net. Operationa1 1imitations led to abandonment of this method of operating, in 1942.

Though one agent was stationed at Dutch Harbor when the Japanese attacked that site by air, CIC personnel were not directly utilized in combat operations; however, the Detachment performed numerous counterintelligence missions closely associated with the Attu and Kiska campaigns, and the combat operations of the Eleventh Air Force.

One of CIC's first tasks in Alaska was to investigate the loyalty of enemy aliens. All Japanese, and those of more than half-blood, were evacuated from Alaska. Loyalty of German and Italian citizens in the area also required CIC attention, as did assistance to Enemy Alien Hearing Boards set up to pass on what to do with these individuals.

CIC made nearly 6,000 loyalty checks of civilian employees of War Department contractors in Alaska, obviously constituting a major portion of their work in this Theater.

The dull and often boring aspects of these cases, though

recognized as of extreme importance, were at times relieved by incidents such as the Fowlie case. In 1944 the 467th CIC Detachment received a tip that a man named Alexander S. Fowlie was going around business and social circles in Juneau, and passing 'himself off as a Brig Gen in the U.S. Army, engaged on a secret mission for Military Intelligence; he showed the star of his rank at every opportunity. A check with War Department confirmed that Fowlie was not even in the military, but was wanted in the states on a polygamy charge, so CIC referred the case to the FBI as the charge was under its jurisdiction.

Many employees had criminal records, so every incident in which sabotage was even remotely possible had to be investigated by CIC. There were many fires caused by dry wooden buildings heated during weather. One $900,000 fire at Adak Station Hospital was traced to a lighted cigarette carelessly tossed into a sawdust pile. A $32,000 fire at an automotive repair shop in Nome resulted from a combination of personnel negligence and malfunction of an oil burner. Fire in the cargo hold of the U.S. Army transport "Teapa" waiting to unload near Seward, raged for 13 hours with extensive damage to ship and important military cargo; its origin was a leaking fuel line.

Although suspicious cases usually disclosed security violations and gross negligence, records up to 1945 do not show a single case in which enemy-inspired sabotage was definite. One incident was probably a sabotage effort, but circumstances prevented obtaining proof; early in 1945 an object believed to be a homemade bomb was found on a troop-carrier air craft in flight; for safety reasons it was tossed overboard immediately on its discovery, thereby precluding an adequate investigation.

The Detachment also had cases of malicious destruction, which looked like sabotage; late in 1944, sugar in gasoline tanks disabled a truck used by a contractor, and a generator motor in the Shemya power plant. CIC pinpointed the civilian employee of a contractor who confessed he had caused damage to "get even" with someone in charge of the truck and the generator.

In 1943 an American soldier was murdered. Liaison Russians in Alaska were suspected but no proof. Among CIC's duties were monitoring the labor situation through an informant network, especially regarding union elements. Other cases dealt with censorship violations, resulting in 50 Courts martial convictions.

Radio broadcasts also were monitored. It was found that standard radios picked up much better programs from stations in Japan than American ones, hence CIC recommended that local broadcast stations be set up at military installations, to insure the reception of our own propaganda, rather than the enemy's.

Recovery of incendiary balloons released in Japanese territory to drift, fall and damage American installations was also a CIC task. In pursuing one of the balloons in January 1945, an agent chartered a plane, and then a dogsled. He recovered the balloon on top of a 45 foot tree, its cargo of chemicals luckily did no damage, no bacteria material was contained in the balloon though that was a fear that had to be set at rest. Several of this type of case occurred.

Dealing with espionage turned out to be largely one of preventive measures. To this end CIC made many security surveys, kept careful control of communications and travel, and conducted careful examination of the personal effects carried by travelers. This paid off in 1944: a departing civilian was found to have a secret compartment in his footlocker – with 87 photographs of newly built runways, aircraft and materiel dumps; 47 of the photos disclosed classified information, none approved by the base censor. "Souvenirs" claimed the employee, so no hint of espionage could be proved; it was not so classified as espionage but the lesser one of security violation.

In September 1944, CIC investigated a food-poisoning case

involving 471 employees of contractors at Ladd Field. Unable to find the cause, CIC learned Thomas Stoeling was in Alaska, he was civilian interned early in the war as a potentially dangerous agent, but was released. He was in the Alaskan theater on a classified project not connected with the army, and in addition had access to the preparation of the tainted food. He did not fall under the jurisdiction of CIC, as set forth by Delimitations Agreement entered into by FBI, CIC and ONI, so his case was concluded by the FBI.

Although CIC in Alaska had no dramatic roundup of spies and saboteurs as in other Theaters, they can be proud that their dedicated efforts probably kept these dramatic things from happening. They were acting to protect backup for our troops in combat, and their work was just as important in the war effort.

XIV

CIC in New Zealand in WW2

BY 1943 U.S. TROOPS by the thousands began arriving in New Zealand to train for combat or rest for 2 to 3 weeks. NZ was thus within the U.S. Army's huge SP [South Pacific] Theater. A need for CIC [US Army Counter Intelligence Corps] in NZ proper was minimal as various government agencies were responsible for civilians and NZ security forces had the situation well in hand. Suspicion of espionage arose mainly from German-Jewish refugees, but NZ covered these and other aliens, maintaining surveillance over those not interned. Most of the work CIC trained for lay in the numerous islands to the north.

So, Why Was CIC in NZ?

Wherever U.S. troops were, CIC agents were also, or nearby. Its agents provided logistical support for Theater HQ in NZ. As GIs increased, some went AWOL or deserted. Due to lack of Criminal Investigation Division [CID] agents, CIC took over finding AWOLs, many hidden by unsuspecting friendly locals. Safeguarding classified information from "loose talk" was a concern centered in 2 areas: hospitals and taverns. To plug leaks in security, agents were planted in bars most used by GIs.

In Auckland, CIC shared an office and worked closely with the host's Security Intelligence Bureau. Unlike elsewhere, CIC's jurisdiction in NZ was mainly limited to U.S. army and air corps, e.g., port security, loyalty and subversive investigations—and security education of GIs, plus some crimes CID would have handled. It also investigated for the U.S. consulate, and escorted visiting American dignitaries on SP theater tours. Eventually CIC in Auckland NZ became the 439th Detachment under SAC [Special Agent in Charge] Edward A. Shevland and four agents.

Undermanned CIC

The first 6 CIC agents into the SP Theater landed June 1942 in the Fiji Islands with 37th Infantry Division shortly after the Battle of the Coral Sea marked the end to Japan's thrust southward. Another scheduled 9 agents never made it. The 37th's General Beightler's appeal on 9 Oct. 42 for more agents brought 2 more, 1 of whom plus 3 of the original 6 then left for OCS; 1 later returned an officer. 37th Division Capt. John A. Burden, CIC Section Chief of G2, had these first agents doing security checks and surveys of numerous military installations.

First CIC officer to take a CIC team over-seas in WW2 was prewar Tennessee lawyer 2nd Lt. Marvin C. Goff, Jr. He arrived with 6 agents Sept. 1942 with newly organized HQ, SP, in French territory: Noumea, New Caledonia. They were redirected to NZ for 6 weeks, then back to Noumea which remained the SP Theater seat until merging with SWPA [South West Pacific Areas]. Known as the SP Provisional CIC Detachment, it covered NZ proper plus the islands north of there, most being French, British or joint territory. The major islands became marshalling yards for millions of tons of equipment and thousands of men headed for SWPA. The prevention of sabotage and espionage fell primarily on this handful of CIC agents.

Cooperation from Islanders

On 250 Fiji islands were 5,000 Europeans. Fiji natives were very loyal to British, many serving in the Solomon's Campaign. Even before U.S. troops arrived, Fiji Police had files on all suspected Axis agents, seized and interned Japanese nationals in NZ and Australia. Summer 1942, CIC searched former Japanese homes for evidence of prewar espionage, finding important data about the area. Some Japanese firms' executives unquestionably sent data to Japan: a Fijian serving with the U.S. Marines on Guadalcanal recognized a captured Japanese officer, "an industrious, unobtrusive tradesman" in Fiji before the war.

Emphasis was on surveillance of local Europeans identified with Japanese and German interests or Petainist, pro-Vichy. An accountant who contributed heavily to the Japanese Navy fund drive before the war was investigated; no evidence was found of spying.

By the end of 1942, New Caledonia was the focal point of CIC in SP, with district offices on the east of the island and the Plaines de Gaiacs and Tontouta Airfields. The Navy had a huge port at Noumea, processing thousands of GIs each month. Natives there were mixed Melanesians sprinkled with whites. [Japanese laborers were deported to Australia early, and a few repatriated. 27 men and one woman were interned at Nouville.

With CIC covering many thousands of square miles, Goff's small unit engaged in observation, surveillance and reporting numerous suspicious persons and incidents in the island commands. He repeatedly asked for help through-out winter of 1942-3, but a worldwide shortage of agents delayed reinforcements.

Some Reinforcements At Last

Goff's pleas finally landed Major Arthur Turner and Lt. George D. Crow with 20 agents in April 1943. Assuming command, Turner and his executive officer Goff worked untiringly months to organize CIC teams at various island commands discharging investigative functions. By year's end, agents covered numbered island commands, plus Noumea HQ, units fighting Japanese on Bougainville, N. Georgia, N. Guinea and Guadalcanal — plus 43rd, 37th, 93rd, Americal Divisions, and 13th AF.

Crow, first CO of IV Island Command [northern islands in New Hebrides Group], was followed by Lt. Wm. C. Wallace who reported on CIC's goal of preventing and neutralizing enemy coast-watchers and subversive natives or agents. Patrolling agents found no evidence to support rumors in winter 1942-3 of Japanese subs sighted near isolated islands in New Hebrides. But searches continued from then on in all offices, for example:

Tahiti-born agent Edgar M. Lucas had been a native labor recruiter in the Fijis, and knew the language and people. He, James W. Franklin and native guide Leon Giovanni patrolled extensively remote Loyalty islands in April 1943 in a navy 50-foot former fishing vessel manned by two enlisted men and a navy warrant officer. The team left Espiritu Santo 21 April visiting Aoba, Aurora, Pentecost, Ambrym, Malekula, Malo, and Vao Islands.

Checking a report from Archdeacon E. G. Teall, Melanesian Mission, Lolowa, Aoba, of a pilot dropping messages in the inland bush, CIC found a NZ pilot dropping love notes to a mission school teacher. They cleared alleged Pro-Japanese Nikolai on Molo Isle, Rene Theyenin and Pere Biguerie, plantation managers on Pentecost, of clandestine radio transmitting.

Another patrol in the Loyalty Group established that a sub had surfaced in Ouvea Lagoon. Similar reports came from later patrols. A monetary reward for the capture and delivery of any Japanese never produced a single one. But Agent Donald D. Ryan in May 1943 on the Isle of Pines, island 30 miles southeast of New Caledonia, reported natives saw a sub on its southeast passage on 16 Feb. 1943. Rumors never produced actual subs, but did confirm attempts of enemy subs seeking fresh water and weather data. Army radar personnel on the Isle of Pines detected a short-wave receiver on two occasions.

A native sail boat carrying uncensored mail to New Caledonia was intercepted, with the uncensored mail confiscated and referred to the Noumea Office of Base Censorship.

On another trip, Wallace and agent Paul Poulin and guide spent 3 days in the interior of Malekula with the Big Nambas cannibal tribe, who had taken pot shots with ancient French rifles at low flying Allied planes. The 2 established a rapport with the Big Nambas with no trouble from them thereafter.

Sabotage

Suspected sabotage cases were few, the most serious occurring in June '43 at the Nickel Co. docks at Noumea, with 52 killed, 115 injured, and large quantities of supplies lost. CIC investigation ruled out sabotage, pointing to improper storage and handling of explosives by inexperienced personnel. Goff, now Captain, was awarded the Soldiers Medal for his heroism at the scene, as he "courageously exposed himself to flying debris and shell fragments to assist in extinguishing large fires and removing valuable government property."

CIC security surveys noted extreme laxity at the American Red Cross Recreation Center, an Air Command Control Room, and several ammo and gas dumps in the Noumea area. The Commanding General sent letters to all faulty installations requiring corrective action.

By 1944, replacements from the U.S. swelled CIC strength to some 30 agents, enabling them to open offices at Hienghene,

Tontouta and Plaine des Gaiacs airfields, with agents Maurice Long, Alfonso Betancourt, and Ralph J. Morin in charge. CIC set up a team at Suva; natives made up half the population, imported Indians the rest; these two races clashed, the Indians being unhappy with the British.

Incoming U.S. troops complicated the situation. Indians began laundry/souvenir businesses for GIs. A pilot hired a family with fourteen kids to do laundry, starting the Orcan laundry handling 160 bundles a week at $2 each, causing Mr. to leave his plantation job. Others followed suit. In 1943 only 2 of 5 sugar mills, essential in wartime, were operating because of conflict between mill unions seeking higher wages, etc. And a rash of fires broke out.

CIC agents and Fiji Police arrested two U.S. soldiers who confessed to bartering U.S. ordnance items for Indian women and liquor. The GIs were court marshalled, given long prison terms and dishonorable discharges. The Fiji Supreme Court found the prime Indian involved guilty, giving him 5 years hard labor. They also uncovered a plot to assassinate the Fiji Governor on one of his inspection trips. The violence, etc., diminished though Indians were troublesome in other subversive ways. A U.S. soldier was found contributing under aliases to the Indian newspaper prior to its suppression. A suspected communist, he was transferred to a forward area to be watched.

Security Checks

October 1942, CIC investigated a globe-trotting Australian prewar ex-school teacher. Her personal effects and diaries gave detailed accounts of military and similar matters gathered from U.S. army and navy officers. It was never established she sent any info to the enemy, but the Fiji Governor deported her to Australia as a menace to military security.

CIC constantly supervised security at airfields and sea

ports, insisting on examinations of civilians as well as soldiers. Censorship violations were common, especially with American Red Cross personnel, war correspondents, USO show entertainers and civilian employees of the War Department. A National Broadcasting Company news analyst was caught with an uncensored roll of exposed undeveloped film with 5 transcriptions in his baggage!

Civilians trying to enter or leave a zone illegally included an Australian merchant seaman on New Caledonia at its Tontouta Airfield. With his British passport were papers saying he was guaranteed work by a Noumea shipping firm. Held at the field while his story was checked, the seaman put on gold bars to enter a nearby officers' club posing as an American officer. When he began hair-raising war tales at the bar, a trailing CIC agent nabbed and took him back to the office. Meanwhile CIC found the firm had never heard of the man. Confronted with CIC's findings, he confessed his passport was forged and he had fled Australia to elude authorities seeking him for several felonies. Agents contacted Australian police, and escorted subject to an aircraft bound for Australia. CIC closed its open file.

In the last of 1943, CIC had to school its agents for a new phase: field security duties. By early March 1944, 2 officers and 16 agents were equipped and trained. Assigned to the 40th Inf. Div. then in NZ, at the last moment they were redirected to the XIV Corps on Bougainville, half to 37th, half to Americal divisions.

South Pacific Loses CIC Agents

All CIC officers and agents west of 159 degree longitude, i.e. Bougainville, 13th AF on Guadalcanal, Munda, New Georgia and NZ, were reassigned to SWPA from SP jurisdiction June 1944. The rest of Turner's CIC was reduced to only agent Charles M. Matthews with the 25th, New Caledonia; others to newly numbered units at SP HQ and on: New Caledonia, Fiji,

Efate and Espiritu Santo, New Hebrides, Guadalcanal, and with U.S. Air Force in NZ.

Rapid Allied advances in the following months further shook up the Pacific commands. On 1 August 1944, the Central and SP Army Forces were merged with HQ, Army Forces Pacific Ocean Areas, with subordinate administrative commands remaining, leaving bases with skeleton forces for divisions resting from severe combat. The only appreciable U.S. forces left in SP were on New Caledonia, Espiritu Santo in the New Hebrides, and Guadalcanal.

Summary

The maximum number in the SP at any time was: agents, 65; officers, 7 — a small force for the vast territory and many islands.

Educating G2s in the proper use of CIC agents was a continuing, worldwide problem in the U.S. Army. In the early WW2 years, many G2s failed to understand the purpose of trained CIC agents. One G2 thought he was getting a clerk and returned an agent with a note the man couldn't even take shorthand! Goff and Turner made it a primary mission to educate G2s in their area.

My service was in Sydney, Australia; Dutch New Guinea, Bougainville, Luzon P.I.

XV

"Ohayo, Gozai Masu"

FIGHTING IN THE JUNGLES of New Guinea, sometimes on short rations but always with the sun blazing down followed by a virtual flood of water from the skies, was the fate of many U. S. foot soldiers in WW2.

Things improved somewhat when they reached the Philippines and found buildings that did not leak, sometimes with an indoor commode and bathtub. But fighting was still necessary for every foot of the way at disputed points. A soldier's life was still grim with day after day of slogging along with his buddies, hitting the ground at the sound of incoming artillery or gun shots.

When atom bombs were dropped on Hiroshima and Nagasaki, soldiers cheered at the thoughts of the war ending and releasing them from the daily grind.

Then the war ended. Soldiers relaxed and looked around for anything to do that was fun. The first troops into Japan for the purpose of occupying the enemy's homeland were in doubt as to what kind of reception awaited them.

My group of CIC agents was with the advance troops of Sixth Army into the unspoiled, unbombed city of Kyoto. We walked from the train station to a nearby hotel where we were to be quartered. As we passed commercial establishments, stores and cafes, we spotted more and more signs in butchered English written by someone trying to learn our language. One of my friends pointed at street signs as we ambled along, calling attention to the fact that along with the name of the streets in Japanese writing were equivalent names in the Roman alphabet. The thoughtfulness of the city authorities in this respect gave us heart.

Arriving at the hotel, our moods were lightened as we found our assigned individual rooms with showers and commodes. No more worries about mosquitoes that used to pester us at night, nor hordes of flies that ruled the days. We were back in civilization.

All of our rooms were on the sixth floor of the hotel, and we were directed to the restaurant on the first floor for our army meals. What a change in diet, we thought. We all went to bed early to overcome the many tiring hours of traveling on the ship from the Philippines and the train ride from the port where we disembarked.

Next morning I arose refreshed, took a shower and dressed in a clean uniform, then stepped out into the hallway to the nearest of three elevators. In a moment I was joined by Mike Horwitz, a Baltimore attorney and our oldest agent. The elevator door opened to reveal its operator: a bright, cheerful looking young maiden of perhaps 18. She held her right hand on the handle operating the elevator as she turned smiling sweetly at us, saying as she bowed from the waist, "Ohayo, gozai masu." We knew she was saying in Japanese the words for "Good morning."

We both answered her with a pleasant "Good Morning." Exiting the elevator we found our way to the restaurant for a good breakfast with coffee and the works. We were well prepared for a good day at the office which had been set up in a nearby office building that Sixth Army Headquarters had taken over completely, assigning different floors for each of its component parts. Our CIC section had a generous amount of space on the third floor with sufficient desks and chairs for each of the five officers composing our CIC headquarters.

As I sat down at the desk reserved for me, I spotted a message lying on top of the table. I pulled it toward me and read that I was to return to the U. S. because of the number of points I had accumulated in my four and half years in the Army.

Mike, the executive officer of the detachment, was reading over my shoulder. When he finished, he put his hand on my shoulder and said, "You are hereby relieved of duty, so don't do a blessed thing from now on. Give me your badge, revolver and your identifying credentials. I want you to really relax; see the city while you wait for your transportation home."

What could I say or do? I decided immediately to make a survey of downtown, and see as many of the sights as possible, using some of the few hundred words of Japanese we were taught in a school in Manila when the invasion of Japan was thought to be our future. Again I noted many signs in broken English, convincing me of everyone's wish to learn our language. I roamed the streets of Kyoto all that day, returning to the hotel in time for chow with Mike and the others. Again I got a good night's sleep, then meeting Mike in the hallway next morning for our breakfast.

We were greeted again by a cute young maiden running the elevator, who bowed politely saying, "Ohayo, gozai masu."

This daily greeting continued for some two weeks from any of the three girls operating the elevators. Then one morning as we sat in the restaurant drinking coffee awaiting our food,

Mike said, "You know, I'd like very much to teach these young ladies how to say good morning in English."

All of us at the table exclaimed, "Go to it, Mike."

Another week passed and Mike said as we approached the elevator, "Well, I think I have finally taught these nice young ladies how to say good morning to us in English."

We got on the elevator and the young operator turned toward us, bowed while holding one hand on her waist, smiled saying distinctly "Oooh, my ack-ing back!"

XVI

CIC Authors Hall of Fame

Books by or about CIC agents and activities

BRAAFLADT, James, career CIC 3923 Summerfield Dr, Pearland TX 77584. Interesting pre-war life, plus CIC career in N. Afr, Italy and postwar. Self-published. Write him.

BRALY, James O., lawyer [Dec'd] 10th Mtn Div CIC Italy, Austria. *Marching with Heroes*, 1948, published after he died, by Ann Braly Jones, his daughter. $29.95, 384 pp hard-cover, Ann B. Jones, 1501 Yarborough, Sherman TX 75092.

DABRINGHAUS, Erhard: *Klaus Barbie*, 1984, Acropolis Books Ltd. Mostly one case by agent involved. This agent also served in early post-war years in Germany.

DUNGAN, Nelson V N, lawyer [dec'd] 32 W. Cliff St. Somerville, NJ 08876: *Secret Agent X: Counter Intelligence Corp*, 1989, Vantage Press.

EDWARDS, Duval A., lawyer, 1421 Minor Ave #617, Seattle WA 98101: *Spy Catchers of the U. S. Army - in the War with Japan*, 1994. Red Apple Publishing, POB 568, Vaughn WA 98394 [now out of business].

FINNEGAN, Dr John Patrick: *The Military Intelligence Story: A Picture History* and others. [Dec/d '02]. Army historian. Co-edited Army Lineage Series on *Military Intelligence*.

GORMAN, Edward: *An American Education* combining personal life before & after CIC service in Hawaii and CBI. Box 1136, E Hampton NY 11937

GREENE, Harris, 3671 N Harrison St, Arlington VA 22207; VA 22207: *The Mozart Leaves at Nine*, 1961 Doubleday. Fiction; CIC detachment. [LOC 60-13735]. Service in Austria 1945-8, with 430th CIC Detachment. Five other books.

HARTER, Hugh A., 25 Central Park West, New York NY 10023: *D'Utah Beach aux Ardennes, itineraires 1944*. 1994, Presses Universitaires de France, Vendome, France. CIC with Patton in Normandy, N. France, Rhineland, and the Bulge.

HAYES, Charles R., 27888 White Rd, Perrysburg, OH 43551, under pen name Manning Spencer: UGF-26 - novel on his CIC cases in WW2 in Germany - self published 1992, (c) copyrighted 1983.

HIRSCH, Richard, M. I., War Dept General Staff in WW2. Professional writer on crimes for 14 years, he fully reported Soviet espionage in North America.

JOHNSON, Thomas M: (Dec'd) *Our Secret War*, 1929. Bobbs-Merrill Company. On CIP and G-2 in WWI [Tom died long ago, was Reader's Digest staff writer, in which he published a number of articles about CIC.

KOEHLER, John O. NCICA #2177, wrote *Stasi - The Untold Story of the East German Secret Police*, Westview Press, Boulder CO 80301. The title tells it all.

KOUDELKA, Edward R., 2200 W. Dickerson #82, Bozeman, MT 59715: *Counter Intelligence: the Conflict and the Conquest - Recollections of a WWII Agent in Europe*; 1986 by Ranger Associates.

LIVINGSTON, Guy [Dec'd], PCB 330, Dobbs Ferry NY 10522, wrote technical, non-CIC articles, and included [1996] his CIC experiences in *Happiness Is*, Eli Gilde, Ltd, POB 330, Dobbs Ferry NY 10522.

MELCHIOR, Ib, 8228 Marmount Lane, Los Angeles, CA 90069: *Case by Case* - published 1993 by Presidio Press, [2/93 GS 15] factual book of his cases in Germany in closing days of war, and thereafter.

MERIWETHER, Frank, writing as Zack Lee Toll, Red Apple, POB 568, Vaughn WA 98394, wrote *South of My Village*, telling a little of his Cold War CIC career.

MILANO, James V., 11136 Pelham Ln, Fairfax VA 22030, *Soldiers, Spies and the Rat Line*, 1997, $23.95. Milano was over 430th. postwar Austria, tells Rat Line story in Cold War. Brassys, 1313 Dolly Madison Blvd #401, McLean VA 22100.

OWENS, William A (Dec'd) *Eye-Deep in Hell* - 1989 SMU Press. First hand account in SWPA and Philippines. Published 14 more before he died; only this on CIC dedicated to Duval Edwards.

PASH, Boris T (Dec'd): *The ALsos Mission*, 1969. Grosset & Dunlap. Contains names of at least 20 CIC agents on this team accompanying army into battle in ETO to detect Nazi's progress with atomic bomb, and pick up scientists working for Nazis.

RICHARDS, Robert R., [Dec'd] 88 E. Broad Street, Ste 1240, Columbus, OH 43210, *Alias "The Fox,"* 1994; Robin Enterprises, Westerville, OH. CIC in N Africa, Italy and Europe; in unit as Victor de Guinzbourg. With 1st team into Dachau with photos along with story of findings there.

SAYER, Ian, and BOTTING, Doug, both in England. *America's*

Secret Army - the Untold Story of the Counter Intelligence Corps: published 1989, Grafton. 1st CIC-CIP world-wide history.

SCHWARZWALDER, John [Dec'd]: *We Caught Spies*--1946, Duell, Sloan & Pearce. First solely CIC book, covers N Africa, Italy and ETO; names censored.

SIMPSON, William Brand: (Dec'd) College Professor. *Special Agent in Pacific, WWII* 1995 by Rivercross Publishing, Inc. Most complete data on CIC cases in Manila in WW2, followed by fascinating cases in North Honshu.

UNRATH, Walter J., POB 3405, Littleton CO 80161-3405. 353 pp, 1997. His army life prior to postwar CIC in Germany. CIC in Berlin. And poem by daughter Alice Jay McKenzie: *The Army CIC - Unsung Heroes, an Epic Poem.*

VAUGHAN, Bradley W, 400 W Baseline #179, Tempe, AZ 85283: *Counterspy Mission in WW2* - published 1993 Vaughan Press. CIC in Africa, ETO and Southern France. Served with famed Victor deGuinzbourg.

WHITE, Bob – Dallas, Texas. WWII Diary about his career in U.S. Air Force, with many photos of plane crashes investigated, etc. Only AF book to date.

WILLIAMS, Marvin: 3620 24th Avenue, Meridian MS 39305. Combining CIC career with personal life: Memoirs of CIC career unpublished, but I have it on tape — DAE

Following is not *by* CICer but is ABOUT a CIP-CIC-OSI agent:

A Spy in their Midst, by Wayne Kiyoshi, 1995, Madison Books, Richard SAKAKIDA beginning with pre-war life in Hawaii before Pearl Harbor, then dangerous life in Manila and career from then on. Get this book!

Part II: Others by CIC agents

BERLE, Gustav: [Dec'd] Ph D, 801 S Ocean Dr #502, Hollywood

Beach FL 33019, books for small business information. In 970th CIC, Vth Corps, Eupen to Pilsen. His quote re Golden Sphinx "It's fun but it stinks."

BRANDT, Dr John H, PO Box 5003, Alamosa CO 81101: books on game hunting, wildlife and man-eaters. *Hunters of Man [2d edition 1995]*, Safari Press, 15621 Chemical Ln, Bldg B, Huntington Bch CA 92649.

CLARKE, Hewitt: 424 Nursery Road, Woodlands, TX 77380. *War Stories from Mississippi.*

CROWN, Dr. David A, 3344 Twin Lakes Ln, Sanibel Island FL 33957: forensic document examining. 430th CIC, Steyr, Upper Austria 1951-3. Kriminalistik Verlad *Forensische Handschdriftenuntersuchung.*

deGUINZBOURG, Victor: Dec'd ETO-N Afr Head of UN Security, friends of foreign nations personnel . Before death published limited edition of letters and comments from them. Robert Richards had a copy.

ENGLISH, James W: [Dec'd]. Before WW2, Associate Editor of Boy's Life, wrote juvenile stories for Boy Scouts. After WW2 wrote juvenile books, eg, *Tops in Troop 10* published 1989.

GIGUERE, Paul E., 24 Brooks St, Springfield MA 01109: *The Stranger,* self-published '96, on OSS '43 & later assignment in France and Germany. Rescued after Normandy landings. Came into CIC, postwar.

Herrington, Stuart: *Traitors Among Us-Inside Spy Catcher's World.* Reviewed 3 GS 1999.

HIRST, Ronald M A "Scotty:" Mathildenstrasse 4, D-65189 Wiesbaden Germany: wrote non CIC. Last: *Three Scenes from Barbarossa.* Trying for agents to share Normandy experiences.

HURLBURT, Arthur, 190 High St. #314, Medford MA 02155: Columnist, *The Medford Transcript*; valuable contributor to *GS and Spy Catchers of U.S. Army*. His work can fill a book. SWPA CIC.

JACOBS, Arthur, Phoenix AZ. *The Prison Called Hohenasperg: An American Boy Betrayed by his Government during World War II* in 1999 on internment of his German parents and himself a native American.

JAMES, Edwin S, 365 College Ave, Rock Hill SC 29730 [born in Portugal], SWPA CIC and Japan. World traveler. Free lance writer, columnist; valuable contributor to Golden Sphinx, NCICA magazine..

KISSINGER, Henry, ETO 84th CIC, Famous not for CIC career. Secretary of State, USA, his book.

OLSON, Fred and Jane, 2437 90th St., Wauwatosa WI 53226. *Dear Jane: a Soldier's Letters [1942-1945]* 94 GS 15. Milwaukee Co Historical Society, Milwaukeem, WISC.

QUALY, Thomas H., 3956 Xenwood Ave., S St. Louis Park MN 55416, trilogy, postwar, about agent in international waters. Ironwood Press, printer-publisher. *Drop Out Zone, The Sand Ghetto and The Bird Dogs*.

RESNICK, Sol, [ETO CIC] as told to Elaine Resnick, Tucson AZ. *Irrigating India,* © 2001. 163 pp. PB Publishing. After CIC, Sol worked in India 1952 as USAID advisor, bringing irrigation to parts of India.

SALINGER, J. D., [ETO CIC] famous CIC author, non-CIC. Many in CIC wrote non-CIC books.

SANDERS, Stephen J., Jr, 7729 E Joshua Tree Ln., Scottsdale AZ 85250, cites CIC: *To Him Who Conquers* published by Fellowship of the Crown, POB 3743, Carmel CA 93921. Subject of book is rare: *theophany*.

SPENCER, Manning: alias Charles R Hayes [see], detective stories, *Murder at Belgrove Country Club*.

STROM, Roy M., 4647 Dead Bear Draw, Hereford AZ 85615: *Dry Lightning*, published 1996. Book of western poetry. $10 each. General Strom.

WARREN, Erika [William Warren], 13 El Quanito Way, Burlin-game, CA 94010, *Life with A Nazi Father*, publisher Red Apple 1994. [2/94 GS 11].

WILLIAMS, Marvin: 3620 24th Avenue, Meridian MS 39305. Combining CIC with personal life: Memoirs of CIC career unpublished, but taped.

19 June, 2007

Specializing in WWII MI Books: CLOAK AND DAGGER BOOKS

Email: Cloakandspies@juno.com, Owner: Dan Halpin, NCICA member

Duval A Edwards, 1421 Minor Ave #617, Seattle 98101, Email: Goldsphinx@aol.com. Please advise if you know of others.

XVII

Chaos in Postwar Japan

FIELD MARSHAL GENERAL SUGIYAMA and wife committed suicide late yesterday as Gen. MacArthur's Counter Intelligence Corps pressed its roundup of the top Japanese commanders who perpetrated the sneak Pearl Harbor attack. Other major developments of the past 24 hours included:

1. General Hideki Tojo, up to late last night. Was given "better than even chance" to live following a direct blood transfusion from an American sergeant.

2. Admiral Shigetaro Shimada, navy minister who planned the Pearl Harbor assault, was taken into U.S. military custody at 5 p.m. yesterday.

3. General MacArthur ordered Japan's nationalistic "Black Dragon" society abolished and its seven leaders arrested.

Marshal Sugiyama and his wife killed themselves with revolver shots at the same time at their home on the western end of Tokyo. Former chief of the army general staff, Sugiyama was closely associated with Tojo and was war minister in the discredited cabinet of Kuniaki Koiso.

Two other suicides were disclosed yesterday. Col. T. Oydomari, public relations officer at the Imperial general headquarters, killed himself with a pistol after poisoning his wife, son and daughter only hours before General MacArthur's order abolishing the imperial headquarters took effect today.

Tanaka Kills Self

A reliable source revealed for the first time that General Seichi Tanaka, a former commander in chief of the Japanese army in the Philippines, also shot himself to death, but the news was suppressed by the Imperial headquarters. A member of the Tojo clique, Tanaka was reported to have asked mutual friends to tell Tojo "shooting is the best way for a soldier to die."

Tojo's condition was described as "very satisfactory" last night by American physicians at the 98th evacuation hospital where the former premier was given a blood transfusion yesterday.

He was removed to the hospital from his home after his failure to kill himself by firing a revolver below his heart as American officers sought to arrest him at his suburban home Tuesday afternoon.

In addition to Admiral Shimada, others on the first list of 40 who were arrested yesterday were four non-Japanese who were wanted for anti-Allied activities. They included Mark Streeter, American civilian, who allegedly participated in Tokyo propaganda broadcasts.

No Resistance from Shimada

The arrest of Admiral Shimada brought one of Japan's Pearl Harbor planners under American custody. The 61 year-old admiral met American Counter Intelligence officers quietly at his home.

He attempted no resistance, and there was no indication of an intention to commit *hara-kiri* despite Tojo's precedent.

A convoy of seven jeeps and an ambulance, in case Shimada attempted to emulate Tojo, lined up in front of the admiral's home at 4:30 p.m., the same time Tojo was arrested the day before.

CIC Major Paul Kraus, who took Tojo into custody, was again in command of the arresting party. The Americans crowded into Shimada's paper-partitioned two-story home on Minami Lane.

The admiral's wife, dressed in a gray kimono, knelt at the mat on the entrance. She smilingly demanded through an interpreter that Kraus show his credentials. They were presented and she then brought back word that the admiral would be ready to accompany the party in 15 minutes.

Kraus agreed to give Shimada the required 15 minutes. While the Americans waited, they could hear sounds of dinner being served. The interpreter, who disappeared along the rear walk, reported that the admiral attired himself in blue kimono, presumably for dinner.

When the 15 minutes expired, Kraus sent a Nisei interpreter into the house to order the admiral to present himself in the foyer. At 4:50 p.m., the admiral, clad in a new but cheap green uniform and a shirt of subdued green tone to match, appeared and spoke to the interpreter in Japanese asking who was the highest ranking officer. Kraus identified himself. When the admiral kept asking questions, Kraus told the interpreter: "Tell him to get his shoes on and get going. Tell him to quit this nonsense."

Shimada did not wait for that to be translated. Placing his hand on Kraus' arm, he said laughingly in English: "Be quiet, I don't suicide."

In a short while, the wife and daughters brought his shoes and dispatch box. The two girls and their mother then formed a semi-circle kneeling behind Shimada. The girls wept silently as they all touched their heads reverently to the mat.

The admiral spoke briefly to his family and joined the cavalcade below, his eyes noticeably moist. He was taken to the headquarters in Yokohama.

XVIII

Story of Richard Sakakida, Hero in War with Japan

THE NAME OF RICHARD Sakakida should be well known to all CIC agents. He was one of the great CIC heroes of WW2, certainly the greatest in the war with Japan.

He died 23 January 1996 after a long illness likely exacerbated by the injuries caused by torture of Kempei Tai in 1942.

CIC officer-agent Ann Bray secured a ten page statement from Dick in the 1950s at Holabird, commenting editorially that he shunned publicity. Slowly in recent years, he has come out of his shell and his story has been told in greater and greater detail.

In Sayer and Botting's first history of CIC, *America's Secret Army*, 1989, the first printed account of Sakakida's CIC experiences appeared. It tells how he and Arthur Komori, another Hawaiian Nisei, were brought into the Army's CIP [Corps of Intelligence Police, CIC's forerunner] six months before Pearl Harbor, then shipped to Manila to uncover Japanese espionage.

There the two posed as civilians, lived and worked in the Japanese community, reporting their findings to MI. Their true identities were known only to a few, until Pearl Harbor made it necessary to bring them into the open with their CIC colleagues. Because of their language abilities, they were invaluable on Bataan and Corregidor, so that MacArthur ordered both to board the last rescue plane and join him in Australia.

Sakakida voluntarily relinquished his space to a civilian Nisei from Hawaii who faced certain death if captured. But Dick refused to admit to the Japanese interrogators, even after severe torturing, that he was an American soldier, successfully claiming to be a civilian compelled by the U.S. Army to help in their translations.

Japanese counterintelligence always had doubts about his story, but could not break it, so he was kept closely watched where he was working at their HQ.

How he survived this ordeal, managed to contact Filipino guerrillas and send valuable intelligence back to MacArthur, is told in greater detail in *Spy Catchers of the U.S. Army in the War with Japan*, published in 1994 by Duval A Edwards, and in *A Spy in their Midst*, by Dick's brother-in-law Wayne Kiyosaki, a 1995 book that incorporates his growing-up years in Hawaii, and his postwar CIC-OSI career.

Because of his being undercover for over three years, and the lethargy of the higher ups in the U.S. army to even consider medal honors for such service, no efforts were made to suitably honor Dick for his heroic service to his country until the last year of his life. Hawaii's Senator Akaka began pushing for special legislation that would enable the Pentagon to suspend its red tape rules regulating the time for medals to be considered.

Your editor joined the efforts of others that included Ft Huachuca's James Chambers, ACICV's Harry Fukuhara, and other Military Intelligence veterans, in assembling data to convince doubting Congressmen that Sakakida was entitled to be specially honored.

There were last minute rumblings from some Filipino veterans who were claiming Sakakida's exploits were exaggerated, and that in fact he had been collaborating with the Japanese. This would be natural for a spy trying to fool the enemy and secure information.

Your editor ran across confirmation of Sakakida's exploits from an unexpected source: a book written by a Col. Hori of the Japanese Imperial Army, published in 1989 by Bungei Shunju. Hori was an intelligence officer stationed in Manila during much of the war. English translation of portions of his book mentions Sakakida by name, and notes that Japanese CI never lost its suspicions of his loyalty, even after they compelled him to sign an affidavit of loyalty to Japan [which one would expect of a spy].

Some quotes from Hori:

> Early Jan. 1945, we received strange information from the counterintelligence division (headed by Major Yoshimi Taniguchi) that had come to Baguio: Sakakida Gunzoku (a civilian employee) who had been used as an interpreter at the judicial affairs dept, disappeared in Baguio. They suspected that he might have been killed by guerrillas somewhere, but they couldn't find him. According to Major Matsue, this Sakakida, a Japanese-American Nisei from Hawaii whose parents were from Hiroshima, seemed to have been around in Manila since Lt. General Homma invaded the Philippines. While counterintelligence was suspicious about him for his close relationship with the American military, they still used him as an interpreter for Lt. General Homma. Sakakida was put in a prison camp as a POW for a while.
>
> But after that, the Japanese army continued to need interpreters. So they made him sign a written oath for his

loyalty to the Japanese military, and judiciary affairs department used him as interpreter to investigate prisoners or Filipinos since the Japanese occupation of the Philippines. Counterintelligence division always had a slight suspicion about him.

After the war, it was found that when the Yamashita troops surrendered and were put in a prison camp, that very Sakakida appeared in front of them in American military uniform as a captain. Major Matsue recalled that moment, saying "I was stunned, like knocked out."

[Knowledge of the Hori book came from a non-member, Stephen C. Mercado, who read *Spy Catchers of the U.S. Army in Japan*.]

The foregoing and other portions of this book by the Japanese intelligence officer were forwarded to Senator Akaka to use in his efforts. Akaka succeeded in having Clinton sign into law on February 10, Section 523 of S.1124, 1996 Defense Authorization Act [P.L. 104-106], that provides a temporary one-year window for application for appropriate awards that were overlooked. For the Army, contact U.S. Army Reserve Personnel Center, ATTN: DARP-VSE-A, 9700 Page Ave, St Louis MO 63132-5200, 314/538-4122

Too late for Sakakida to know about, but not his relatives and widow.

Your editor received this letter dated 15 February 1996 from Daniel K. Akaka, U.S. Senator:

> Thank you for the tremendous support you and others have provided in this important endeavor. I urge you to make every effort to ensure that your fellow military intelligence veterans are informed of this singular, limited opportunity to seek long overdue recognition of their contributions to national security.

Efforts to get Congress to award a Congressional Medal of Honor to Sakakida were unsuccessful. But he was authorized the second highest medal, and also a building at Fort Lewis, in the state of Washington, was named in his honor.

XIX

The Story of the Security Intelligence Corps

SUSPICIONS OF RUSSIA CAUSED CIC to keep tabs on communists in the army. Suspected Army officer Joseph Lash was under such surveillance in 1943. CIC agents trailed him to a hotel where he got a room next to one reserved by *Eleanor Roosevelt*. Meeting was taped. Lash spent the night with Eleanor's secretary, which CIC didn't know then.

As a case of joint jurisdiction, a copy of the tape was delivered to FBI who played it before our President. The roof fell in: with no positive proof Eleanor was personally involved, an irritated Roosevelt ordered Army Inspector General to investigate G2 and CIC. Lash was immediately ordered to somewhere in the Pacific as were two CIC agents [names unknown]. Result: Inspector General ordered CIC schools and world HQ closed and ALL records destroyed, CIC taken from G-2 and agents in ZI [Zone of the Interior] placed under Office of Provost Marshal General.

December 20, 1943 War Department ordered all Service Commands to consolidate Intelligence and Security under the Provost Marshal General now charged with supervision of *all* investigative functions in ZI. In January 1944, 963 remaining

CIC agents and 900 OPMG agents were officially combined into SIC [Security Intelligence Corps], mission: loyalty investigation of military and civilian personnel in military and vital war industries; cases of suspected subversion, sabotage, espionage, disaffection and disturbances that might require use of troops; agents authorized civilian clothes unless uniforms required.

Luckily, 19 January 1944 General Eisenhower requested 473 CIC officers and agents for the coming liberation of France and Europe, and MacArthur continued requesting agents, saving CIC as a separate organization outside CONUS [continental U.S.]. [OPMG agents outside of CONUS continued as CID.] Others saved in ZI were 162 CIC agents with Manhattan Project, 718 with Army Air Forces [including Air Transport Command], 516 with Army Ground Forces training for overseas. Unexpected and undesirable: outlawing CS [Countersubversive System], a valuable source of leads for CIC. Later in January '44, 169 more Service Command agents were taken to fill the quota going to ETO.

February 10th 1944, Col H. R. Kibler stepped down as Chief, CIC. Col. Wise took over and closed Baltimore World HQ for good on 15 February 1944, with records destroyed per Inspector General orders. Thirteen staff men were transferred to D.C. to CIC Branch of Counterintelligence Group, Military Intelligence Service, WD.

At the operational level, the feeling each group had for a special type investigation was *officially* eliminated but in reality both CIC agents and OPMG agents continued doing what they had been trained for. Most CIC agents remaining in ZI had no chance to attend CIC advance and specialized schools before they closed.

One would think that all existing badges and credentials were replaced solely by SIC ids. Not so. No living agents of either CIC or OPMG recall exchanging their own for new credentials, etc. Most were unaware of the combined groups, though some did note a change in leadership.

Major A. E. Peters, CO 2d Service Command, wrote: economy of combined operation as expected by Inspector General's report was questionable because of the severe blow to morale of both CIC and OPMG [also known as Internal Security Division] agents, with a virtual paralysis of investigative activity in Service Commands between October '43 and March '44. Peters also said this six-month period was a prime target and last chance for enemy subversion before the Normandy invasion, as Service Commands had the barest handful of trained agents to meet such emergency. Luck was with us while the crash program combining two different organizations seriously lowered our level of security from October 1943 until war's end.

Major Peters further wrote: several factors were involved in lowering the morale of both former CIC and OPMG agents, but the merger was superficial as missions and jurisdictions of both were merged into Security Intelligence Corps, the chief difference being the organization's name of SIC. New agents coming in received SIC credentials and badges and were trained by schools, including former CIC ones, run by Provost Marshal.

The effect of the Inspector General's report eliminating CIC schools was not considered serious *at the time*. It was believed ZI SIC would be kept at full strength by new processing men through the former CIC school in Chicago under SIC auspices.

In August 1944, combat units going overseas needed more agents but unavailability of men left many units in ETO and Pacific undermanned. To meet the demand, a course was started at Camp Ritchie which satisfied current needs. With redeployment of ETO CIC Agents to the Pacific after V-E day, stateside CIC began to revive: a new CIC school was set up at Ft George Meade MD under a newly designated CIC Chief. The CIC Center, abolished February '44, had transferred training functions to Ft Meade; in September '45 it was revived at Camp Holabird MD.

From 1945 SIC agents were trained through Fort Holabird. In May 1945 Service Commands were again authorized CIC detachments. SIC gradually decreased to 512 agents.

11 March 1946, the Director of Intelligence recommended 206 officers and 306 EM SIC in Service Commands be merged with CIC.

WD Circular 108, 13 April 1946, rescinded Circular 324 of 1943, and transferred *all* SIC personnel to CIC, removing all traces of the decentralization of CIC caused by the Inspector General's report effective 1 January 1944.

15 April 1946, 602 SIC provost marshal credentials were revoked and replaced by CIC badges and credentials.

On 18 April 1947, by Special Order #77, the War Department named Brigadier General George V. Keyser the Commanding General of the CIC Center and Chief of CIC. Successive chiefs included Brigadier Generals E. A. Zundel and J. K. Rice until August 1951.

SIC in 8th Service Command merits special mention: its combined CIC and CID agents worked well together. Replacing MI's Col Rolfe, OPMG Col Pond led all agents in Texas, Louisiana, Oklahoma and New Mexico together effectively. One of its last official acts was participating with other Service Commands providing guards for United Nations forming in San Francisco.

Returning to Texas, 8th SIC agents decided to maintain contact with each other on resuming civilian lives. They immediately organized in 1945 the SIC Association comprised solely of CIC and SIC agents who worked at any time in 8th SC. This first CIC-SIC club still exists today as SIC, meeting once a year somewhere in its former territory. No distinction is made between CIC, SIC or former OPMG agents.

One noteworthy exception to the usual practice of most

other groups is that very early the spouses and relatives of CIC-SIC agents in 8th SC's SIC were invited to join and participate in all activities, which they have done, preserving the group.

The SIC is now held together by the daughter of former agent Judge John Compton of Houston TX, Catherine Compton who puts out a monthly newsletter to all members. In recent times, *any* former CIC or SIC agent now living in 8th territory is invited to join as associate member. Annual dues are very low. Miss Compton, known as "Cat," can be contacted by Email at catcompton@windstream.net.

XX

Japanese Fifth Column in the Philippines

US SOLDIERS LANDING AT Lingayen Gulf, Luzon, 9 January 1945, marched toward Manila. An estimated 5,000 fifth columnists were burning towns, demolishing buildings, and shooting at us on the way. These Filipinos in Japanese uniforms could change into civilian clothes and pass through our lines as refugees with little effort.

Reports of this have been meager. Most Filipinos were either neutral or loyal to the US. Many turned more anti-Japanese the longer the war lasted.

Ganaps, Sakdals and Makapilis formed this fifth column. Hukbalahaps "Huks" [Tagalog for ("The People's anti-Japanese Army")] were another group, another problem. A few other small groups were not large enough to do harm. Who were these dissidents causing us problems? The dregs of troublesome prewar groups.

The Sakdal Party

Before 1930 Benigno Ramos, clerk dismissed for insubordination in Filipinos' Senate, organized illiterate laborers and peasants of Central and Southern Luzon against his political enemies. He proposed a platform against American rule including complete independence, with no control nor American influence, and return of Philippines to its oriental heritage *under Japan's guidance*. In 1930 Ramos started *The Sakdal* [Tagalog: "to accuse"] a paper for his Sakdalistas followers. In 1934 he traveled to Japan from where he sent propaganda.

May 1, 1935, an uprising surrounding Manila ended with many leaders arrested. Efforts to extradite Ramos from Japan for trial didn't succeed. Revolt leaders testified some actually expected Japanese soldiers to help. Some found guilty of subversive activities were released with a pardon by the American governor-general. Uprisings continued in Luzon. Ramos started a new group called Ganap with same Sakdal aims and programs.

Ganap Relations with Hukbalahap

Certain parallels existed between these organizations: both drew members from peasants and laborers of central and southern Luzon; both favored agrarian reform; both wanted immediate complete independence for their country. There the parallels ceased. Huks were strongly anti-Japanese; Ganaps strongly pro-Japanese.

In 1942 certain Ganap leaders approached the Huks to invite cooperation for agrarian reform and the Greater East Asia Co-Prosperity Sphere. Huks refused; they preferred to be what their name spelled out: anti-Japanese -- and did so to the very end and beyond.

By 1939 Ramos left Japan to take up his program in person. Evidence indicates he was commissioned to set up an espionage system for Japan. He was interned in 1939 for subversion. After Pearl Harbor, two thousand of his known followers were quickly picked up and interned as security risks. It's a safe bet CIP's [CIC] "Lost Manila Detachment" participated in this roundup. Japanese freed these Ganaps and others including Ramos, when it took Manila.

As Japanese occupation began, there were an estimated 400,000 Ganaps, mostly in Luzon. Ramos offered them to serve Japan. But December 8, 1944 Japanese combined the three parties into one national party called Kalibapi [League of Patriotic Filipinos] with Ramos a director. He also was forming Ganaps into military and labor unit organizations for Japanese to spy on guerrilla activities.

General Artemio Ricarte and Pio Duran joined forces with Ramos. Ricarte "the Viper" was a leader of the Insurrection against the Americans led by Aguinaldo. In 1901 he entered Manila to start an uprising and was captured. Refusing to take the oath of allegiance to the US, he was banished to Japan where he continued to write propaganda for distribution in the Philippines. He also maintained contact with some of the secret societies; in fact he was the head of one called Tangulan in Bulacan, formed in 1930 to start a new Philippine Republic. After the fall of Manila, Ricarte returned triumphantly with the Japanese.

Pio Duran, a political opportunist, perceived the Ganaps to be a quick way to power. His knowledge of what went on in the presidential Malacañan Palace proved valuable to Ricarte and Ramos.

In 1943 the Japanese began training Ramos' Ganaps in guerrilla tactics and intelligence methods. Some 10,000 Filipinos received basic military training attached to Japanese units. Some were selected for training in Fort Santiago for espionage and sabotage.

Puppet President Jose P Laurel declared war against the U.S. in September 1944, enthusiastically greeted by the Sakdal-Ganaps. When Laurel decreed against conscripting Filipinos to fight with Japanese against Americans, he was accused of having made a hollow declaration. Japanese officials in Manila cooled on Laurel and openly courted Ramos, Ricarte and Duran, who offered Ganaps under their command, promising more recruits. They wanted a Filipino Army called "Kalipunang Makabayan ng mga Filipino" shortened to Makapili.

Founding the Makapili

Founders present at its inauguration: Laurel and other puppet dignitaries, e. g. Ramos, Ricarte, and Duran. General Yamashita presence showed Japan's sanction.

Political circles in Manila believed Laurel attended fearing its formation was a try to take his power away – proved to be true. The trio promised Yamashita 60,000 Filipinos with a voluntary enlistment of 20,000 each month. By now they had 80,000 Ganaps with some training from which to build their army. Had the U.S. not advanced so rapidly, it is likely the trio would have replaced Laurel.

Makapili Objectives

Those who have minimized collaboration by Filipinos should take a closer look at Makapili objectives. The Philippines was "bound to shed blood and sacrifice lives of her people with other East Asians in order to eradicate Anglo-Saxon influence in East Asia;" and "collaborate unreservedly with Imperial Japanese Army and Navy in the Philippines."

These were from the propaganda machine in Tokyo. The concern of Americans, especially CIC, were the number of Filipinos fighting for Japan, and betraying fellow Filipinos loyal to the US. By VJ day, CIC had over 5,000 in prison charged with everything from treason and betrayal of downed U.S. pilots, to open and willful collaboration with Japan against the interests of the Philippine Commonwealth and US. Had power and mission of CIC not ceased on VJ day, many more would have been investigated and imprisoned.

Makapili Accomplishments

As announced 8 December 1944, Makapili was intended to be a Philippine Army, on an equal basis with the Japanese Army. Its trio of leaders became major generals, and other ranks were to equal those in Japanese Army. Makapili soldiers were to be outfitted by the Japanese and trained both as regular soldiers and espionage agents and saboteurs.

Many partially trained Ganaps were eager to become Makapili, but recruitment failed expectations because of lack of time and Japanese inability to feed and equip them. Also retarding recruitment were conflicts between the trio. Estimates of the final Makapili strength were ten to twenty thousand. January 1945 one thousand well-trained, well-equipped Makapili were stationed at Christ the King College in Quezon City. Similar detachments were reported elsewhere in Luzon.

Japanese officers did not trust Makapili in combat as separate detachments. Most were assigned to Japanese units. This was an affront to Makapili leaders, who could do nothing about it for after this new organization was formed, retreat from Manila of its leaders began. Americans landing on Luzon 9 January 1945 aborted Makapili recruiting and nullified its command. Makapili soldiers were left with Japanese units they were attached to.

It is difficult to determine the aid Makapilis gave in defending Luzon. Makapili organized resistance crumbled before the Americans arrived, reducing them to sabotage and espionage. But elsewhere—Bulacan, Rizal, Laguna, and Tayabas—they fought alongside Japanese soldiers. Many Makapilis were killed in combat; more surrendered with Japanese, or deserted to surrender to Americans. Hundreds were still fully armed when surrendering.

Makapili were more valuable to Japanese in espionage and sabotage. The large number of displaced civilians roaming the provinces, coupled with small numbers of CIC agents, made screening almost impossible. As a result Filipinos went between combat lines with comparative ease. As Makapili were trained to infiltrate, some were captured with maps of American positions or other incriminating evidence on their bodies. Some carried passes actually identifying them as spies! We were hampered in detecting some because we were forced to rely on other Filipinos for clues and information. Few Filipinos would betray close friends or extended families [large by our standards].

Proof of sabotage by Makapilis was less difficult. Captured ones confessed to the burning of Tarlac and Camp O'Donnell, as well as destroying buildings and key bridges. Makapilis were the cause of much of the demolition and burning in Manila.

US policy on Makapilis & Ganaps

We had sufficient evidence to justify declaring Makapilis enemies, so those captured would be prisoners of war. Instead, each case was judged individually, resulting in many guilty of the worst forms of subversion being released without punishment. It was impossible to investigate thoroughly all those captured; there were too few CIC and too little time before the war ended. When Makapilis surrendered or were captured, they claimed they were forced by the Japanese as most all Filipinos charged with collaboration said. Too frequently this plea was accepted. Leniency to Makapili soldiers gradually developed; near the end many were released on surrendering.

Ganap and Makapili leaders were investigated more thoroughly. By VJ day a number of them awaited trial by the Philippine Commonwealth on charges of treason, though too many were cleared of subversion. Feeling was strong among U.S. soldiers exposed to bullets fired by Filipinos. Loyal Filipinos were also dismayed at soft treatment of Makapilis and Ganaps; they felt every Filipino caught wearing a Japanese uniform should have been executed.

The Sakdal-Ganap-Makapili were crushed. Ramos and Ricarte were dead and Duran interned on treason charges, as were many others. The majority, concentrated in an area filled with trouble and social unrest for at least a generation, never stood trial.

CIC lost its authority to arrest as of VJ day. U.S. turned the task of punishing the 5,000-plus charged with subversive activity over to the Philippine Commonwealth government on 2 September 1945, with all control in the hands of the Commonwealth Government, even though it was not yet well established.

The U.S. was out of it on 4 July 1946 when the Philippines gained complete independence. But CIC was around for as late as 1947, gathering loose ends and additional evidence in connection with trials in Japan and Manila. This CIC unit was the 1135th, which we can say is the "Last CIC Manila Detachment" — putting a final ending to the "Lost CIP Manila Detachment," which lost all but three or four of its members in Japanese concentration camps or in combat.

The source for this was the accumulation of papers in GS editor's possession. It could have been written by Walter Hauboldt, an erudite CIC Special Agent; or by Special Agent William A. Owens in his collection of CIC memorabilia now in a special section at Texas A & M University. I have made slight changes in a few places for cosmetic effect, and updated it as much as possible.

– Duval A. Edwards

XXI

38th CIC Joins in Liberating Bataan and Corregidor

By Alexander Kozak and Duval A. Edwards

Bataan and Corregidor

These two words will endure as long as the Day of Infamy when the Japanese made its sneak attack on Pearl Harbor. Thousands of Filipino and American GIs died in the Bataan Death March followed by deadly prison camps. They will not be forgotten. Courageous defenders struggled on Corregidor Island until General Wainwright surrendered. They will not be forgotten. Richard Sakakida and Arthur Komori, CIC Hawaiian Japanese-Americans, will not be forgotten for their work on Bataan and Corregidor, and undercover work in Manila.

Kozak trod along much of the same ground they had covered, unaware of the heroism of these early CIP-CIC agents, who had rendered important translation and interrogation service to starving loyal Filipinos and out-numbered American soldiers fighting and hoping for help from the U.S. that never came. In turn Kozak rendered CIC service important to our troops in recapturing Bataan and Corregidor.

THE HUKS, SHORT FOR Hukbalahap, were a communist guerrilla outfit on Luzon that fought the Japanese invaders. While not shooting Americans after we landed, they were taking over town after town in certain areas by installing Huk leaders to replace elected officials after executing them.

Many communities on Bataan were terrorized by these merciless Huks until CIC reached the scene. The 38th CIC with the liberating 38th Division had its hands full with a group of 9 Huks led by Maximo Crimen around Marikina in Rizal province. Loyal Filipinos said this group of nine Huks was the most interesting case of those who had brutalized citizenry of the community. During the investigation the name of Maximo Crimen came up in every instance. He committed the most violent acts — the worst was drilling a hole in the victim's shoulder with a drill bit.

38th CIC arrested the whole bunch, so Maximo was finally in custody. Contrary to the "ogre" picture given of him, he was as meek as a lamb, readily confessing to all the allegations against him. His name was expected to be a nickname, but he insisted it was his real name, and he was so booked on the report as well as in Bilibid Prison where prisoners were held.

Japanese had defeated us badly on Bataan and Corregidor in 1942. Kozak was proud to be a CIC agent with the 38th Infantry Division in retaking both Bataan and Corregidor in 1945.

Before the Bataan operation the 38th Division was reassembling from its operations on Leyte where it campaigned in combat along with elements of the Xth and X1th Corps. Its next mission was to protect the right flank of MacArthur's Sixth Army on Luzon Island.

Kozak came into CIC in November 1944 while at the Replacement Depot, Lae, New Guinea. From Lae he went to CIC Hollandia school, then to the 38th CIC detachment with the 38th Division preparing for its Luzon operation.

To show CIC status, brass letters "US" were pinned on their caps and shirt collars just like officers. It was very effective in letting agents do their job.

Kozak's first duty as an agent was educating line companies with CIC's job, as well as the value of turning captured Japanese documents over to CIC or ATIS [Allied Translators-Interpreters Section].

The 38th Division under XI Corps landed on Luzon at Zambales coastline at 8:30 a.m. on January 29, 1945, 20 days after Sixth Army forces landed at Lingayen. Kozak went in with the 2d Battalion, 151st Regiment—unopposed as the enemy did not anticipate this landing on Bataan, putting U.S. troops on the right flank of the Sixth Army as it marched on Manila, with most of its soldiers totally unaware of the 38th protecting its right flank.

CIC duties were light at first. Checking loyalties of potential washerwomen made GIs very happy. Checked out a farmer looking for livestock who was first suspected of spying. An important job on CIC's list: cautioning officers about leaving maps and plans unattended.

38th CIC found a suitable HQ in a house in the middle of San Narciso, on Rte #7 to Olongapo and Zip Zag Pass. They could see our troops going south from the staging area, then returning shaken and bedraggled. Agent John R. Murray went down that road with his assigned line battalion and returned white as a ghost, stammering for days afterward. One night Japanese had infiltrated its perimeter and killed a soldier in a foxhole next to Murray's.

The 151st Regimental Combat Team was formed and prepared to depart Olongapo, Bataan, on February 14th. The enemy succeeded one night in penetrating its perimeter and blowing up one of the artillery spotting planes. Kozak was assigned to the 151st on the 12th. Goal: amphibious landing at Mariveles [close to Corregidor] on the 15th.

The Mariveles landing was relatively uncontested, though a few incidents took place. Further inland the enemy mounted a counter-attack but was beaten off. Next day resistance stiffened in the hills.

A large amount of rice had been found. CIC's job was directing it into the hands of hungry civilians as it collected information from civilian informants.

A combined amphibious and airborne landing assault on Corregidor Island by the 503rd Airborne and the 3rd battalion of the 34th Infantry Regiment took place on the 16th. With combat in final stages Kozak's 2nd battalion of the 151st Infantry relieved the 3rd battalion on February 25th, 1945.

When Kozal arrived on Bataan bodies of dead Japanese due to the heat were in advanced stages of putrification with flies everywhere. Only by shielding food with one hand or helmet liner could one take a bite not covered with flies.

The whole of Bataan was liberated in 19 days; associated Sixth Army actions around Manila Bay took until April 16th. Then Kozak was relieved of line operation duties and returned to division CIC HQ. His duties were now occupied with investigating collaborators.

When the detachment moved to Iba, Zambales province, in early March, work continued on collaborators. Assisting the team was a group of guerrilla officers until it was discovered they were implicated in the killings of Captain R. McGuire and Sergeant O'Hare, American soldiers who had been operating with the guerrilla force during the Japanese occupation. This was a serious turn of events, requiring full investigation. Unfortunately, it was still unresolved when Kozak was reassigned.

There were plenty of cases for CIC. In addition to those assigned to him, Kozak was given the responsibility of covering the northern area of Zambales. One unusual case was that of an alien Chinese in a barrio along the China Sea. He had been aboard a Japanese ship when it was sunk by one of our planes.

To interrogate the Chinese, Kozak had to use an interpreter for English to Tagalog, to Pangasinang to a Chinese dialect and then another Chinese dialect — then reverse the flow. Other than Lt. Alec DeCastro, all the other necessary interpreters were found in that one barrio!

38th Division relieved the 6th Division by May 5th. The 38th CIC took over from 6th CIC the two story palatial home of the Gomez family, in Marikina, Rizal province. It now encountered a new risk: Hukbalaps, Ganaps and Makapili. The Huks were anti-Japanese as well as anti-American; Ganaps and Makapili were fighting alongside and for the Japanese, which had not been seen in Zambales. If a Filipino was one of these, he automatically merited checking out.

Kozak was so busy that in a letter to his girl friend back home [who he married after the war], he wrote "just received four major cases and eight minor ones, and am working twelve hours a day."

As the war drew near its end, talk of rotation abounded. Kozak had eighty-eight points – more than needed. When Japan surrendered he had to decide to stay in and go to Japan, or return home. He chose the latter hoping to get a good job. Jobs were hard to find in Cleveland when Alex was discharged from the Army Oct. 26, 1945. He gave up intentions to return to college when Cleveland advertised for policemen. Studying for the job, he took the exam and placed 38 out of more than 600 others. Eventually he joined the Cleveland Police Department and did very well.

From the beginning July 16, 1946, in 4 years he rose to Sergeant, then Lieutenant in 1961, to Captain in 1966, Deputy Inspector in 1972 until retiring in 1983 at age 64. When he was Captain of the Fifth District, he said he had turned from fighting the enemy from without to fighting the enemy from within, as the area was rampant with crime and black nationalists activities including sniping at police. His police tour included doing many new innovations, such as simplifying IBM computer terminals so personnel could easily work with them. Experience in CIC played an important part in his police work, he believes.

Kozak and his wife, Catherine Connell of NYC, had two girls and two boys, all married and giving their parents thirteen grandchildren.

XXII

Where Were You X Years Ago?

1946

WE HAVE NO RECORD of any newsletters devoted to CIC in this year. This deprives us of usual sources for stories, but the memories of all who had been, or were being, processed out of CIC in this period, are as fresh and reliable sources as any.

Most were concerned with putting lives back together. Many went back into the practice of law; others sought new fields, and a number pursued a higher education. A few remained in service or returned to it.

We have since learned those still in CIC had their hands full in the occupation of former enemies. More and more Nisei were trained and brought into the corps to enable our troops in Japan to forestall the USSR's efforts to convert the Japanese government to a communist society.

Agents were in the final stages of completing and testifying in war crime cases, not only in Japan and Manila, but also in Germany and a number of other spots around the globe.

In the absence of newsletter sources, we look to you in CIC in 1946 to share tales of your labors. Until then, we'll select some of the choice stories in newsletters from 1945. The only newsletter then, to our knowledge, was *The CIC Record* out of the 441st, Manila PI. Regretfully we have only parts of June 15 and August 25, 1945 [all marked "Confidential, to be destroyed after perusal"] in our possession. This item shows the work CIC continued to do:

CIC Agents Arrest 12, Smash Million Peso Manila Bay Plot

CIC agents in May arrested 12 men, seized 5,200 pesos and took into custody and safekeeping a hoard valued up to 15 million pesos. This wrote the climax to a yarn involving buried treasure and undercover operation.

Agents John J. McQuillan and Robert C Harrison, acting on an informant's tip to the 493rd, infiltrated a ring bent on illegally recovering treasure from waters off of Corregidor; it had been dumped in 1942 in wooden cases by the army, which had collected all available silver and gold bullion in Manila but were unable to ship it as planned by sub to Australia.

The two agents were on board the ring's barge on May 17 as it moved to the treasure site and its divers went into action. As buckets of silver were being hoisted, an undercover agent of another organization cooperating with CIC hung his shirt over a railing, a signal acted on by a cutter half a mile away with CIC agents aboard. The 493rd's Major Carlos P. Marcum had followed the action from a Piper Cub, and landed to take a small cruiser to the barge with a search warrant.

Shortly, CIC had all members of the ring under arrest, the treasure confiscated and Coast Guard ships patrolling to prevent further theft until the treasure could be properly recovered.

1970–1

Louis W. Farley, who had served in the 487th with James F. Conway and its CO Dudley G. Skinker in the Philippines in

WW2, died in Framingham MA. He was the presiding judge, First District Court of Southern Middlesex, active in legal and civic organizations - and a long-time member of MIANE.

Mike Sydorko, elected National President, began putting out the welcome mat for NCICA national convention scheduled for 31 July-2 August, in Washington DC.

Major General William H. Blakefield left the command of USAINTC on 28 Feb. 1970 to head KMAG, the Korean Military Advisory Group. NCICA hosted a luncheon at Holabird on 19 Feb. where he was given an Honorary Life Membership certificate.

Beginning of the End

What many believe was the initial blow in 1970 that caused Congress and army brass to deliver the knockout punch to CIC by 1971 arose out of a series of articles in the media on Army Intelligence and counterintelligence activities. Written by a former faculty member of the Intelligence School together with a former member of the 116th MI Group at the time a reporter for the *Chicago Sun-Times*, they were considered as serving to defame, degrade and impugn the integrity of the Department of the Army and MI.

Only Senator Hruska's voice called for a sensible, thorough investigation into the allegations - but the politicians then in Congress refused to listen. Other media failed to investigate. All this hubbub caused Congress to pressure the Army, and Army Top Brass caved in. The result as one CIC agent still in the field overseas recently put it, "the demise of CIC and the infamous 1 June 1971 letter [Army's doing away with CIC as a separate unit] .... cut our legs off."

Some CI managed to hang on since then, but CIC as we knew it was no more. But in more recent years there is evidence that some key people in the Army understand the need, and some form of CI has slowly hobbled back into existence.

It is not a separate unit that performs as CIC did, however. In fact, it takes more than one organization to deliver the goods that CIP-CIC delivered with a meteoric rise in recognition from established organizations such as the FBI, ONI and other agencies.

XXIII

CIC Special Agent Richard Sakakida Rescues 500 Filipinos Held by Japanese

SAKAKIDA WORKED UNDERCOVER IN Manila months before Pearl Harbor, pinpointing Japanese spies. When MacArthur left Manila for Corregidor, Sakakida went along as interpreter. When MacArthur was ordered to Australia to reorganize forces against the enemy, he ordered Sakakida there also. It is not generally known that Sakakida gave up his place to get away to a civilian Nisei helper [with family in Japan] who faced death by Japanese as a traitor.

Sakakida voluntarily put himself in the same dangerous spot by remaining on Corregidor. But he knew that his mother had the foresight to remove his name from an earlier entry in the consulate's records, which if left there would have put him in the same danger spot.

When General Wainwright surrendered and left the island of Corregidor, Sakakida was separated from the GIs on Bataan, and turned over to the Kemper Tai. Every conceivable torture known to man was used by his captors in an effort to make him confess he was in the U.S. Army—and thus a traitor due execution. He told his captors the truth except for that one fact: knowing it spelled his death if he admitted it.

After months of torture, the Kempei Tai finally turned him over to Japanese Army HQ then in Manila. He was placed as a clerk in the Adjutant General's office under watchful eyes. Unsuccessful attempts were made to trick him into disclosing he was an American soldier.

Things were not entirely quiet on Luzon, the main island to the north of Leyte. Sakakida had a most interesting 1944, as he continued to watch carefully for more traps. Then came the real big break that he had been awaiting:

One day the wife of Earnest Tupas came to the Judge Advocate General's office and asked Sakakida to translate for her a request to visit her husband who had been captured and confined to a 15 year sentence in Muntinglupa Prison. Sakakida knew that Tupas had formerly worked with Manila CIC agents, and since Bataan fell worked with the guerrillas. Sakakida revealed his identity to her, filled out passes for her and many other guerrillas' wives with forms he stole from the office where he was still permitted, assuring her she need have no fear using them at the prison since Japanese prison guards couldn't read English anyway.

Mrs Tupas, knowing many guerrillas with her husband, was able to arrange meetings between them and Sakakida during his "free hours" after last bed check and before early morning one. With them he made a plan to free Tupas and 500 others confined in the prison. Not the normal duty of a CIC agent, but nothing was normal at this time in Sakakida's life.

He told her to advise Tupas to get a job with the prison electrical department so that at a designated time he could short-circuit electrical facilities, and to get word to other guerrillas to case the prison for the best time for a break. The report to Sakakida was: prison officers made a security tour each night between midnight and 2 a.m. Sakakida next had the free guerrillas obtain Japanese officers' uniforms in order to carry out the devised plan.

On the big night Sakakida left his barracks after bed check. He and our local guerrillas, all dressed as Japanese officers decorated with ribbons with swords clanking at their sides, approached the prison's main gate. Thinking "officers" were making the nightly security inspection, in accordance with Japanese custom the guards bowed low in respect — and found .45s stuck in their ribs. A tap on the head put them out of commission for a while. Out went the prison lights on schedule and some 25 guerrillas overpowered the rest of the guards and released nearly 500 Filipino prisoners! Sakakida hurried back to his quarters in time to make the 6:30 a.m. roll call. While he worked in the colonel's office the next morning the Superintendent of Muntinglupa Prison dashed in to report the break. The colonel hit the ceiling, dismissing the Superintendent.

Shortly after the breakout, Sakakida contacted Tupas now in Rizal mountains with the other guerrillas and had radio contact with General MacArthur's HQ. Now Sakakida had a means of relaying a vast amount of information picked up around the colonel's office, particularly data on Japanese troop movements and shipping activities. One most important contribution was part the plans for a Japanese Expeditionary Force to Australia. Some months later he learned what happened from a JAG officer aboard one of the 15 vessels that had left the Philippines with plans to land at Port Darwin; he returned to the Philippines on the only ship that got back. U.S. submarines and air planes had taken care of the rest.

In December 1944, the Japanese Fourteenth Army HQ moved to Northern Luzon because of heavy air attacks on Manila; in April 1945 moved further inland. Feeling growing hostility toward him in the headquarters, Sakakida decided in early June 1945 to escape to the hills. In a week he joined a small band of guerrillas in the vicinity of Farmschol. Ten days later they took a severe shelling in which Sakakida was wounded and left when the guerrillas escaped.

Left alone, Sakakida treated his wound and survived almost like a savage in the jungles until he spotted strangely uniformed soldiers speaking English. MacArthur had issued orders to be on the lookout for his favorite interpreter. Sakakida, only known Nisei held prisoner by the Japanese, had rescued himself, and served many more years in the Army.

XXIV

Jerry A. Alajajian

Only CIC agent arrested and escorted manacled in chains back to Theater HQ to face Court Martial for disobeying in combat a lawful order of his Commanding Officer. If found guilty: death

SHOCKED, CIC SPECIAL AGENT Art Hurlburt watched in amazement at the two MPs leading a tall, well-framed man in handcuffs to MP HQ.

"Impossible! A CIC agent under arrest? I can't believe it!"

Looking closer, he recognized the man! It could only be, and was, CIC Special Jerry A. Alajajian! Art was in Hollandia, Dutch New Guinea [now Irian], in the fall of 1944 training for General MacArthur's promised return to the Philippines.

As soon as he could, Art visited Jerry at MP HQ to find out what could have brought about the unheard of — a CIC Special Agent arrested and handcuffed?

Jerry briefly stated he was charged with disobeying a direct order of his Commanding Officer in combat, and was being taken to CIC Theater HQ in Brisbane for Court Marshal.

The last time Art had seen Jerry was when they landed together in February 1944 with agents off the "Sea Cat" vessel from San Francisco, USA. They parted on separate assignments. Both from Massachusetts, they had served a period of time in the First Service Command, Boston HQ.

Born in Armenia in 1914, Jerry Alajajian was a small child when the Turks solved their Armenian problem by means of genocide. His parents with two small boys escaped with their lives, reaching America in 1919. In Massachusetts, one of the two boys was Jerry who grew up to be 100 percent American.

After entering the service and applying for CIC, his background was thoroughly investigated back to his first days in the US. He met all the tests: capable of talking at least one foreign language, exceeding the minimum age of 25, mature, discreet and not associated with any organizations on a certain list; his IQ exam when inducted was more than ten points over the required minimum IQ 110 for an officer. The conclusion: perfect for a CIC Special Agent.

As will happen, two lives touched each other again and again during and after WW2. Hurlburt of Boston first met Jerry at "808," the old Cadillac dealership building beside Cottage Farm Bridge on the line between Brookline and Boston.

During the war it was headquarters for the New England area CIC. Jerry was processed into CIC at Ft Devens, while Art came from Coast Artillery at Harbor Defenses of Narraganset Bay.

There were then some 350 agents at "808." Jerry and Art met usually at Physical Training sessions on Wednesdays. Jerry was voluble in his hatred of Turks, there being no good Turk except a dead one, he opined. He claimed to have a long, curved knife at home, not to be unsheathed without drawing blood. If anyone wanted to see it, fine - but would have pricked fingers to keep the tradition.

After summer of 1942 each went his own way, never crossing paths again until early 1944 going over seas. As Army logic would have it, Jerry wasn't sent to the Near East where he was familiar with the languages, but to the Southwest Pacific. The two met at Ft Meade, staged for overseas, rode the train to San Francisco, boarded the "Sea Cat" and set sail for Brisbane, Australia, in a shipment of 130 CIC agents under officer-agent Dudley Skinker. This group became known as "Skinker's Stinkers."

Unloading from the "Sea Cat" in Brisbane, they marched to the city's outskirts to a tent city set up in the middle of Ascot race track. The next morning at reveille, roll was called by a tar-heel sergeant with no experience with non-Georgia names. He called "Brown, Smith, Jones" to a chorus of "here's," but stumbled on Jerry's name. First he said, "Allah—, Allah—" then gave up, spelling the name out, slowly, letter by letter. A deep voice from the rear rank piped up, "What initial, please?" [Two and a half years later, at the initial get-together of CIC veterans at Elk's home in Brookline Village, Massachusetts, Art spotted Jerry across the crowded room. Loudly he shouted, "What initial please?" Jerry knew instantly who was being called and who was doing the calling.]

From Brisbane Art went north to New Guinea first, to Finschhaven, while Jerry went to the 41st CIC detachment with the 41st Infantry Division.

In April 1944, the 41st Division had moved from Finschhaven, 600 miles up the coast of New Guinea and freed Hollandia for the Dutch, enabling MacArthur to take another giant step on the road to the Philippines and Japan. We were sitting in our tents waiting to board an LST to liberate another Japanese held position a few hundred miles up the coast: Biak Island. Jerry joined us along with several other replacement agents bringing our unit up to strength. He made a vivid impression as he showed his famed Armenian sword resting in its fancy scabbard.

We outguessed the Japanese by landing on Biak several miles from where the enemy thought we would. The only opposition to the landing was from a dozen Zero fighter planes diving at us on the beach. We managed to dig fox holes and escaped deaths, while our anti-aircraft batteries, set up quickly in anticipation, brought down most of the attacking planes — aided by some of us shooting from our fox holes at the low-flying planes.

Biak turned out to be a hornet's nest, with most of the enemy well concealed in numerous caves lining the shore all the way up to an air field that was the division's first objective. Artillery fire, including good sized cannons, stopped the advance of our troops up the coast, splitting some off, so it took much tactical planning and fighting to reunite with them.

During the several weeks this fighting went on, most of our CIC unit was stationed near Division HQ at the landing site where our CO, "Texas Jack" Y. Canon, spent much of his time. After a couple of weeks, Canon began leaving the camp in his modified jeep with a machine gun mounted over the front hood. We knew from observations during the Hollandia operation that he was really searching for souvenirs, which he proudly brought back and handed out to the growing number of officers who appreciated these gifts. Nice souvenirs to send home to families!

As senior CIC agent I was Canon's first sergeant, known in CIC lingo as Special Agent in Charge; I set up my portable desk where unit records were keep on a daily basis. During this period of relative CIC inactivity, I learned Jerry's story well.

Few CIC agents were trained in I & R work [Intelligence and Recognizance], but I was. When Canon began ordering an agent to go somewhere, they started coming to me first. Sometimes I said it was not within the scope of our work, other times it was. Why I was not in Jerry's shoes, handcuffed and facing Court Martial I'll never know; but when stationed elsewhere and hearing of Jerry's situation I felt I may have caused Jerry to be in the spot he was in, and offered to attend the hearing on his behalf. He did not answer, and obviously did not need me.

Jerry's story to the Court Martial Board was: while he had told his CO to go to hell, he had good reason for it in his mind. He had been ordered out on patrol for seven days straight, while others in the detachment only went once. In addition he had just received news his brother had been slain back in Boston; he was frustrated in not being able to comfort his parents at such a time. And he felt the patrol was not a lawful order, outside the scope of CIC duties.

The commanding officer who brought the charge, Canon, also known as Cactus Jack, did not fit the mold of a CIC agent in our unit's opinion. We felt he was misplaced and should have been in a fighting outfit, not Military Intelligence.

Many at Brisbane HQ knew about Jerry's CO and believed Jerry's story. The colonel who headed Theater CIC told Jerry not to worry but due to the serious charge a Court Martial was compulsory.

As the colonel predicted, the Court cleared Jerry and all its members went to Jerry to shake his hand completely ignoring Canon. Via the grapevine, other agents heard he had beaten the rap but details were unknown until after the war.

Canon never realized the caliber of agent he was trying to condemn. Jerry was returned to CIC duty in Australia, then to the 43rd CIC [43rd Division] under CO Ray Hodgson. From its 9 January 1945 landing on Luzon, Philippine Islands, to 26 February, Hodgson assigned Jerry to establish and maintain liaison with a group of guerrilla intelligence agents to obtain tactical and counter-intelligence information. At times Jerry and his detachment worked in an isolated barrio with no combat U.S. troops nearby, with Japanese soldiers infiltrating the barrio, some in civilian clothes mingling with the civilians. Guerrilla Captain Diego Sipin became ill and asked Jerry and another agent to take charge of his battalion. Jerry obliged.

At times coming under artillery and small arms fire, plus nightly infiltration, he directed the guerrillas in locating and neutralizing enemy artillery, plus securing sketch maps of the enemy's troop dispositions. And thanks to liaison with his guerrilla unit, Alajajian was responsible for apprehending two notorious enemy collaborators for which he was awarded the Bronze Star.

On 16 May 1945, Alajajian was with an officer and an enlisted man in a jeep, trying to cross Angot River in Luzon. In mid-stream, the wheels of the jeep dropped into a hidden hole overturning the vehicle and throwing all into the water. The officer could not overcome the swift current and was being carried down stream when Jerry spotted his trouble and immediately went to the rescue, pulled the officer to safety after the current had carried them more than a hundred yards. For his thinking and initiative above and beyond the call of duty in a non-combat situation, Alajajian was awarded the Soldier's Medal.

Jerry went on to become President of the National CIC Association the host of the 1960 convention in Boston, with 600 members attending from all over the country. In civilian life he became a top executive of Boston Mutual Life Insurance Co., reaching the highest position – president.

In September 1944, I was stationed with the 214th CIC attached to XIVth Corps Headquarters on Bougainville in the Solomon Islands when news of Jerry's arrest reached me. I immediately wrote Jerry, offering to testify in his behalf; no reply came, only news that the Court Marshal had ruled in favor of Jerry. I relaxed but didn't hear the specifics until many years later.

XXV

Looking into the Past

IN 1945, CIC REACHED maximum strength worldwide [estimated at 3-5 thousand], as well as peak effectiveness in safeguarding our army from enemy agents and subversion [uncounted thousands except in Philippines where over 5,000 awaited trial].

After the conflict with Germany ended, CIC regained its right to have its own CIC chief, with headquarters and training facilities back in the States where Roosevelt had temporarily broken it up as a separate entity for almost two years.

While some detachments were poised or on their way to help in the final fight with Japan, CIC under MacArthur were planning for and anticipating the roughest most costly landings to date on the shores of Japan proper. The Okinawa campaign was a precursor - and the native Okinawans were not all the loyal Japanese as those on the home islands.

The dropping of the A-bombs brought a great cheer from CIC agents awaiting the coming Operation Olympic, the final invasion.

The perceptive ones foresaw the end and began changing from combat plans to an overall counterintelligence operation. When surrender was announced many hearts and minds gladdened with visions of final safety and the chance to return home to pick up the threads of interrupted lives.

Despite the Pentagon's belated efforts to retain a substantial corps of experienced agents to deal with postwar problems already being encountered in ETO by tendering direct commissions, the great majority of former lawyers, investigators, news reporters, etc., chose to bow out. A few remained to face different challengers -but that is a story or stories for later.

Air crash on Okinawa killed 5 CIC agents on way as first CIC into Japan: Oscar W Keys Jr., Roy C. Allmond, Donald R. Soper, Gail Gaines and 11th CIC Det CO John H Norton [for whom Norton Hall, Tokyo, was named]. The lives of 10 accompanying Nisei were also wiped out.

CIC in Germany was assigned the task of liquidating the German Army General Staff, all intelligence and police agencies and all known leaders. This was reported in August 1945 by John F. Somerville Jr, CO of the 221st CIC Detachment.

1970

In 1970, CIC was basking in the success of its efforts over several years in reporting to authorities on the riots in the 1960s that swept our nation, causing death, disaster and destruction in some of our largest urban centers.

Normally outside the jurisdiction of CIC, the extent of the civil unrest had overwhelmed local and state authorities as well as the FBI and other federal authorities. The aid of CIC, which by then had attained the utmost respect for its effectiveness, was sought and granted under the authority of the President as Commander in Chief of our Army.

As recorded by Ann Bray, the publication of articles by a former faculty member of the School at the Bird, together with a reporter [formerly with the 116th MI], had brought about a crisis for CIC. The Army was charged with "spying" on American civilians. "Unconstitutional" screamed the headlines. The politicians in Congress took advantage of the situation to make hay for themselves, all but Senator Hruska that is, who called for hearings on the allegations. Hruska was ignored, there were no hearings, the Army was simply told to desist spying on civilians.

While the disastrous results did not take place until the following year the machinery was in place. Nervous top Army officers quaked in their boots at fears of a hostile Congress and caused MI to wipe out CIC again much as Roosevelt had done in 1943 - except now it was the final blow.

As one career agent on duty overseas then wrote "the MI letter of 1 June 1971 cut off the legs of CIC."

Perhaps a more apt phrase might be: "it blinded an eye [or eyes] of MI and the Army?"

Peepholes into the Past 1970

Otto Fiedler, Chairman of NCICA's Board, reported membership to be over 2600, and growing.

MG William H Blakefield left the command of USAINTC in February. At a luncheon in his honor at Fort Holabird, NCICA President Michael Sydorko presented him with an Honorary Life Membership in NCICA.

NCICA held its 23rd national reunion in Washington DC 31 July, 2 August. Gordon M. Kingsberry was elected National President, and Atlantic City was announced as the choice for the 1971 convention. Special Agent 1942-6, Gordon became VP at the First Pennsylvania Bank of Philadelphia. His widow Lois has brightened many NCICA conventions even to this date.

A new chapter was reported forming in upstate New York, with Sylvester LeDoux, and Emerson Laughland [of Watertown] prominent among the organizers.

BG Jack B. Matthews was announced as the new chief of CIC.

Bernard J. Sweeney continued his analysis and reporting on communism in the pages of the GS.

Included in news items from members were notes from: William Hartnett, Ted J. Girouard, R M Penn.

Included with the hardworking members who passed away: Frank Krauser, George W Morris.

Order of the Unsought Laurel

Awarded to Jim Marion for extraordinary loyalty and devotion to the welfare of NCICA, in recognition of a severe case of writer's cramp from mailing over 100 letters promoting the national convention to names on his personal list.

Jim Conway, Towson MD writes:

Talking to Bob Stahl, coastwatcher who addressed a recent CICAM meeting, I mentioned I had known of the cargo sub Norwhal bringing evacuees from PI and New Guinea to Australia, as a CIC team was debriefing them to compile our black/white lists. I think they were at the 85th Station hospital. Stahl wonders if we have any record of that CIC unit's work? Names of some we questioned?

Stahl is writing about 3 Americans who sailed from Mindanao to Darwin, Australia, arriving 4 January '43. They were Charles M and Athol Smith, and Jordan A Hamner. I can't remember the CIC team, but Bob McCormack may have been one. I worked with them only part time; I lived at the Atcherly Hotel, Brisbane, a few blocks from the Lennon Hotel.

Stahl has searched the MacArthur Library, Norfolk VA without success. He asks if any of our members can recall where the three men were questioned, where the records may be?

Looking forward to Colorado Springs.

[Jim, how about Andy Anderson? Since CIC records were destroyed, with many mingled in G2 records, zeroing in on a particular incident in which CIC performed has been almost hopeless. Sphinx]

XXVI

Muscle Shoals Case

DOWN THE BEAUTIFUL TENNESSEE River near Florence, in northwest Alabama, was the Muscle Shoals dam, where in peacetime fertilizer in the form of phosphate and nitrate was fabricated by means of the hydroelectric power there from the Tennessee River. In wartime, this source supplied an important ingredient used in the manufacture of ammunition for our armed services, thus plants involved in the process and all civilian employees came within our jurisdiction. Atlanta had received a report from overseas of defective, unsafe ammunition emanating from a plant that used the Muscle Shoal product; little pieces of iron filings were found inside the ammo.

I was ordered to investigate, and afterwards relocate my one man office to nearby Florence to cover northwest Alabama. The investigation was practically completed by a concerned, responsible management by the time of my arrival. But I had to make an official report, so they led me step by step through the entire facility to follow the process. One of the final steps was sifting of the nitrate through a metal screen to kept out foreign objects and large clumps. Any chemistry student knows that this product isn't particularly friendly to metal, and gradually eats it away, thus the screen generally deteriorated in time, and became less effective, allowing bits and pieces of its metal to break off and fall into the finished product.

Not so much a problem in the manufacture of fertilizer, but could be, and obviously was, in making powder for our shells. Management was already aware of the cause and had already replaced the old screens. I could discern nothing that indicated anything more than negligence, and so reported to Atlanta. In a case like this, all employees who had anything to do in any of the steps were checked out by CIC for anything in their background that would indicate disloyalty, or even disaffection. I heard nothing further on the case, and assume nothing instigated by enemy agents was uncovered.

My handling in the investigation must have impressed someone at Atlanta HQ because the next thing that happened was I was transferred to the office at Annistan AL that covered eastern and northern Alabama, as well as Fort McClelland near Annistan. There I would experience two interesting investigations into possible espionage and sabotage.

XXVII

Anniston Hotel Case

THIS MUSCLE SHOALS CASE apparently brought my name back to the attention of the Atlanta office, for after a stay of only a few days, I was transferred to Anniston AL, to what had been a one-man office with Henry Ingargiola of Baton Rouge LA in charge. After I replaced him, he was on his way with his Italian language ability to the first combat CIC teams in our North Africa landings, and later to Italy.

Now it was no longer a one-man office. Nearby Fort McClellan, a munitions storage facility and a number of air corps installations in eastern Alabama caused it to be increased to three of us within months. In addition, we continued the protection of the arsenals at Huntsville. The Florence and Muscle Shoals area was handled by agents out of Birmingham, under the direction of Major Fuller who after WW2 ended was temporarily head of the Air Corps CIC, later to become the Air Force's OSI [Office of Special Investigations].

In most cities we managed to find free space in a post office. Here in Anniston, however, we occupied a room in a regular office building, with lettering on the door to proclaim we were an insurance agency. No one ever opened the door to inquire about insurance. With help now, I assigned routine cases to the new agents, while I maintained contact with the PIO at McClellan, and a nearby munitions storage facility [its PIO George Hamner later came into and served in CIC many years].

While stationed in Anniston, we received belated confidential news that on the eastern coast on June 12th two German submarines landed eight trained saboteurs with missions to destroy plants in New York, Philadelphia, Illinois and Tennessee We were ordered to insure that networks were in place around all army facilities that would report anything and anybody suspicious immediately. Outside of some purely innocuous reports, we heard nothing, though we made certain we had covered every possibility.

It was not until after the war was over that I learned all the Germans who landed had already been captured by the FBI even before we got our first alert of their presence. The powers that be didn't see the need to advise us of that, as there was always the possibility of other such invasions by enemy agents bent on sabotage. And indeed there was: on November 29, 1944, a U-boat landed two agents at Crabpoint ME, with espionage and sabotage orders. Their mission was too little and too late. It was aborted quickly when the one who was an American ex-sailor turned himself in, and helped the authorities capture the other, highly trained, operative.

But finally in Anniston I ran into the real thing in my specialty of spy catching. Two cases came along, the first being a mere warm-up for the second. Just before Christmas, an officer at Fort McClellan reported to the PIO that he had been approached at a hotel in Anniston by a young lady under very mysterious circumstances. He felt that she had mistaken him for someone else she was supposed to meet, so he played along with her as she asked him searching questions about what was going on at the Fort, like troop training, identity of units, troop movements. The PIO and I agreed that the officer should continue the contact and report to us daily on further developments.

As this looked like it might involve an army officer and a civilian contact who was not an army employee, it was obviously a case of joint jurisdiction with the FBI. I notified the local FBI, and on the day after Christmas a team of three FBI agents was camped in our CIC office. By agreement, and as proper, they began an extensive background investigation of the female, while we huddled with our army officer, and gave him elaborate instructions on questions he should pursue and actions he should take. At the same time the PIO tightened up his internal organization for greater alertness to a possible spy on the post. [In a short time, it paid off!]

Thereafter this became a daily ritual: we met with the FBI, who used our office to report by telephone every morning directly to J. Edgar Hoover, while we prepared our normal daily reports to our Atlanta HQ and Birmingham offices, listing our activities. We conferred with the FBI daily on plans for that day and night, and relayed the information our officer was providing us. And of course we were trying through the PIO's own informant network [every army unit had such a counter-subversive system, called CS] to try to determine the identity, if true, of that unknown officer the civilian subject had intended to contact.

As our army officer continued to have dates with the suspect night after night, we knew in advance where he planned to take her. The FBI agent in charge then asked if one of us could get into our army uniforms in order to get closer to the subject and officer. They wanted an independent witness other than the officer, if possible, to every word that was spoken by the suspect. It was a logical enough request as almost everybody in the night spots was in uniform, and unhappily for them FBI agents looked like FBI agent. I dusted off my uniform, borrowed a second lieutenant's bars from the PIO, and made a date that enabled me to sit unobtrusively not too far from the suspect at the bar or dinner, where she was taken on the date.

While all of this was interesting, especially as it lasted through New Year's Eve, the FBI agents and Hoover were becoming more and more perturbed with the lack of any solid information on such an ideal setup for an espionage ring, even though they had thoroughly checked the hotel staff and found nothing to substantiate any sign of a ring. And our continued efforts to confirm the identity of a subversive army officer turned up nothing.

I was not surprised therefore when the FBI voiced their desire to check the living quarters of the subject. As she lived alone in a house with no landlord, to gain entry meant forcing an illegal entrance, which of course the FBI would never do, at least on the information so far obtained. But the mission of the CIC was to prevent harm to our armed forces, so after listening to the complaints of the FBI another day, one of my agents was able to gain entry and invited the FBI to join him. After this inspection, FBI picked up the female for questioning. The final report absolved the subject of being anything but an intense reader of detective and spy stories, with nothing to indicate any connection with anything like an espionage ring; she had been having fun and dates at the expense of the Army!

I cannot recall which one of my agents did FBI's work for them, but that ended this case which proved to be a training refresher for the next, more serious one.

XXVIII

Fort McClelland Nazi Mechanic

IN THE MEANTIME, ON one of the visits to Fort McClellan, my PIO introduced his new assistant, a major who had just come into the army from his civilian job of mayor of one of the Alabama cities. As usual, the PIO introduced me as Mr Edwards, never revealing my rank [he probably knew] then of a tech sergeant. The following week I made a routine call on the PIO and found he was out, leaving his new assistant in charge.

The major asked me in to the office, put his fingers to his lips and spoke softly so the soldier clerk in the outside office couldn't hear, "Can I ask you a very confidential question?"

I closed the office door and nodded assent.

"Please tell me, Edwards, what does G-2 mean?"

So this tech sergeant told the G-2's new assistant, a major, exactly what G-2, G-1, G-3 and G-4 meant, all the time struggling to maintain my composure as I, an enlisted man, had to educate a man who had somehow managed to gain entry "the easy way" into the army as a major. All the while, the thought popped into my mind, "Whatever happened to that proposal in Congress to grant CIC agents officer or warrant officer status?" [I eventually heard it was voted down to keep the "army from rewarding unqualified civilians with easy commissions!" Ha!]

Following the farcical case of the "Lady in the Hotel" which had so perturbed the FBI, our biggest case of suspected espionage up to then came along -- entirely within CIC's jurisdiction. Through the PIO's network at Ft. McClellan came a tip on a civilian employee of the motor pool. This information may well have come as a result of the PIO's tightening his CS system following the hotel-lady case.

There was no evidence of foul play, only suspicions caused by the fact that the employee always immersed his fingers in weak acids long enough to continually obscure his fingerprints; coupled with the fact he was a loner with a German name. Not enough to get alarmed at, but as taught in our training schools, pass up no reports. After all, the FBI had broken the submarine saboteur ringers the year before within a couple of weeks by paying heed to a single, innocuous phone call.

Hence we opened a file on our suspicious acting army civilian employee; the further we went into his background, the more interesting and suspicious it looked. As leads we sent out to other sub-offices, especially in Florida, brought data back, we discovered that our subject—now upgraded to suspect—before the war had been convicted in Federal court of smuggling between Cuba and the mainland. He was now on parole, so why should he worry about obscuring his fingerprints? Possibly doing so, of course, had allowed him to being hired as a mechanic at one of our busy camps, where thousands of troops were being trained and then shipped to overseas destinations. A perfect spot for a lower grade German spy.

What did we have on him that warranted an investigation? The fingerprint concealment was enough for us to continue prying, to see what he was doing in his spare time, who he kept company with, who he was writing to, and why he continued to obscure his fingerprints.

Under these circumstances, we instituted a mail cover procedure on him through the post office, to discover the names and addresses of those with whom he was corresponding, but of course we had no legal right to read the contents of the letters. For the moment, we made no effort to interview his co-workers, as a careless slip could alert him to our investigation. So after the routine of checking records of all kinds at the county courthouse, police department, credit bureau, as well as similar checks back in Florida, our next step was to shadow him as he left work, see where he goes and who his contacts were.

Using the handy walky-talkies the PIO procured for us, with an agent in each of two cars we tailed him for three nights in succession, while one of us sat in our downtown office as a control center. On none of these nights did he return to his rented room. The first two nights he stayed at one address, the third night at an entirely different one. Our neighborhood checks indicated our suspect was quite a lover—either had two girl friends, at least, or was a bigamist. The morals of the man did not concern us at this point, we were intent on whether he maintained any kind of contact with any person to whom he might conceivably be passing troop information.

A survey of his living quarters was now definitely in order. Swearing his landlady to absolute secrecy, we borrowed a key to his apartment while he was on the job at the camp. We went through every scrap of paper there, leaving everything as we found it so as not to alert him. What we found though, aroused our further suspicions: newspaper items had been clipped out and filed in a folder of other mementos. Most of the items concerned the exploits of a German general on the Eastern front fighting the Russians—and the last name of that general was identical with our suspect's! This coincidence definitely intrigued us. In passing, we also noted four new tires still in their wrappers, for which special permits had to be used under the wartime rationing then in existence for such products in short supply. We found no authorization for their purchase, nor record of same at OPA [Office of Price Administration] in charge of issuing them.

We redoubled our watch over the man's activities, though we didn't have the manpower to do so 24 hours a day, seven days a week. Here we solicited the aid of his co-workers certified loyal by the PIO. We interviewed and instructed them a safe distance from subject. It was now a game of watch and wait.

Days passed, weeks passed. Nothing through the mail cover; the man simply didn't write, nor receive intriguing mail, nor did he ever leave town on trips. A mail cover on the ladies with whom he kept company had produced no further leads, either. No change in his routine at night, where he favored one address a few nights, then another, then back to his apartment a night or two to rest.

The war went on. We had other cases, nothing as serious as this number one threat of espionage. Troops completed training at Fort McClellan and were moved out, and still no movement by the suspect. After conferring with my supervisors at Atlanta HQ and Birmingham, we finally had to face the fact that our primary mission included the protection of our army from *potential* threats. We didn't have to catch them in the act or with evidence to present to a jury as the FBI did. Nor did we have sufficient numbers of trained agents to maintain surveillance forever. Therefore, we did the next best thing under the circumstances, which was to neutralize him until the war was over. With what we had on him, this was easy enough to do.

One afternoon as he was exiting the gates of Ft. McClellan, with one of my agents in the background, an MP made the subject get out of the car while a search was made. As we suspected, from the glove compartment the MP brought out a pistol, the possession of which alone was sufficient to cancel his parole. In addition, however, we were able to present evidence of the illegal possession of the tires which were secured without the required permit, which enhanced his prospects for a longer prison life.

While not entirely satisfied, we were content in that we had utilized all of our CIC training in neutralizing for the duration a potential threat to our armed forces. There was no doubt in our minds that if and when the suspect had the chance, or was contacted by a professional enemy agent, he was certain to betray our country. The subject's parole was revoked by a Federal judge and he was put behind bars to serve at least for the duration of the war.

XXIX

Case of Airborne Death in Training

THE LAST CASE OF any importance that I was involved in was when I was stationed in Columbus GA where Fort Benning is located. I was SAC of a four man office, myself and three agents: Carl F. Savino of New York, Carter O. Lowance, a newspaper reporter [after the war, secretary to the governor of Virginia], and Robert C. Josey III from Scotland Neck NC.

When French General Giraud visited the States in July 1943, he made an official visit to Fort Benning. Our office had the job of ensuring his security during the visit. This began with the PIO insisting on lending me a first lieutenant's bars, while I got into my soldier's uniform. He had offered captain's bars, as I was to be in command not only of my agents in uniform but also of MPs and other soldiers in providing the security detail. I declined, as I suspected no one would believe my baby face could warrant captain's bars. I accepted the first lieutenant's bar.

We cleared of anti-French bias those working in the areas the General would be quartered and come into normal contact elsewhere. On his arrival we preceded his official motor entourage around the camp with two agents in one jeep, followed by two in a second jeep; we repeated this the following day as he visited a demonstration site and made a few comments in French, complimenting the demonstrators. At each location we visited troops were drawn up in formation, saluting Giraud as he passed; we could not help but enjoy returning salutes as a share of honor bestowed on this general.

The case I alluded to involved the training of paratroopers. They had to practice jumping from as great a heighth as possible, which turned out to be jumping from an elevated platform holding a wire rope attached to a high pole. The rope was long enough to reach a few feet above ground, giving the soldier enough clearance to jump the last distance when the wire rope reached its length.

One day, an unfortunate trooper used the wire rope but it came loose as he plunged toward the earth so that he died from the unexpected impact.

The question in all such incidents was: was it sabotage or negligence on the part of someone? From my experience at Muscle Shoals Dam, it took a brief time before I found where the wire rope that worn through the metal loop to which it was attached, and when the trooper's weight was suddenly added, it broke at the worn spot, causing the trooper's death.

An investigation of all involved in the maintenance of the equipment satisfied me it was simple negligence on the part of the crew maintaining the setup. So I reported and closed the case.

XXX

Some CIC Outstanding Cases

1943: U.S. ARMY COUNTER Intelligence Corps announced 19 December it had exterminated a Sicilian Fascist organization, dedicated to sabotage and other subversive acts against the Allies. It was financed by a daughter of one of the island's wealthiest families.

Fifteen young men and the girl were arrested at Trapani, after a two-month investigation. Cataldo Grammatico, 20, was the self-confessed leader of the group. He was a second year Palermo University student and former section chief of the Gioventa Italiano Littorio [Fascist youth group claiming 7,000,000 members].

The organization, called "Fedelissimi Del Fascimo" [Committee of Those Faithful to Fascism], was the first cell of a group designed ultimately to reach throughout Sicily and Italy. Members swore: "In the name of God, of Italy and of the Martyrs of my idea, I swear to give myself to the cause of those faithful to Fascism." Only one arrested showed any regret at having joined. Two admitted actual acts of sabotage.

Wealthy "angel" of the society was Maria D'Ali, 22, law student at University of Rome, member of all Italian youth organizations, daughter of the vice federate of the province of Trapani. She confessed to participating in a meeting of the organization, and to planning propaganda on behalf of the group.

First clue of the organization was Oct. 14 when CIC agents found on Trapani buildings bulletins protesting conditions, denouncing President Roosevelt and claiming lack of bread, oil, clothes, shoes and work. The manifesto ended with: "Long live revolutionistic Sicily." The accused faced the death penalty, but less harsh a punishment was indicated.

1944: CIC arrested over 100 Italian spies and saboteurs operating for the Germans in Allied-occupied Italy since the first of June; 16 were executed, Allied Advance Force HQ announced. The majority were "left behind" in Rome when the Germans pulled out; CIC also made arrests in other parts of the country.

Twenty-eight among those listed are in prison awaiting trial on espionage and sabotage. "German authorities have relied throughout on quantity rather than quality," it was stated. "By dispatching large numbers of ill-trained agents, Germans sacrificed 95 percent in hopes 5 percent complete their missions.

"This policy proved disastrous. Almost every spy arrested has talked freely and given the Allied authorities particulars of other agents with whom he was trained or whom he saw at one of various German intelligence stations. The following warning was issued to persons who have accepted missions into Allied territory on behalf of the Germans or who are considering accepting such missions:

"We probably have your name and description on our list. If you are already in liberated Italy we are searching for you. If you are about to come we are waiting for you. You are advised to give up at the first opportunity. *Those who have been executed did not give themselves up. All those who have given up are still alive.*"

1945: Two Caught by CIC/SIC Convicted William Curtis

Colepaugh, an American, became a traitor. In November and December 1944, he and a German, Erich Reich, were caught in the act of lurking in and about U.S. army and naval posts, camps and forts for the purpose of espionage, sabotage and other hostile acts. All for the purpose of passing their information on to the German Reich.

Using false names and wearing civilian dress, they thus clandestinely passed through the defenses of our installations to perpetrate their conspiracy — until CIC/SIC agents uncovered their activities and secured evidence of their conspiracy.

Arrested, they were tried 6-14 February 1945 by a military commission at HQ Second Service Command, Governors Island NY, presided over by Col Clinton J. Harrold, with Maj Robert Carey, Jr, JAG, serving as trial judge advocate.

Charged with "Violation of the Law of War, Violation of 82nd Article of War, and Conspiracy to Commit all of the Above Acts," they were found guilty and sentenced to be hanged.

President Truman later commuted the sentence of the American to one of hard labor for life; and on the end of WW2, did likewise for the death sentence on Reich.

Thus another chapter in the exploits of the SIC-CIC is brought to light with the help of CIP-OPMG-CIC-SIC agent James N Marion.

....

Clark A BARRETT, Esq, San Mateo CA:

"During the Korean War I was a CIC agent, and have been a life member of NCICA since 1979. It appears to me we are hypocritical to our own values in the court-martial of Lawrence Rockwood for his actions in Haiti. I've read [he] was simply on an intelligence-gathering mission to the prison. I believe NCICA should support this mission.

"I am not attempting to pre-judge the proceedings; however, how can we appear other than hypocritical when we denounce human rights abuses abroad, and yet court-martial an Army [CI] officer merely seeking to ascertain the truth concerning [such] abuses in an area controlled by the U.S. Army?" [Many of us agree with you, Clark. More writers and publications do also, one being an article by Meg Laughlin published in Tropic [Florida] 1 October; earlier ones by Col. David H. Hackworth for King Features. Sphinx]

W. Bradford CHASE, Jr., Boston MA:

"RE 7th CIC [3/95 GS 12], correct spelling is MOHAR, not Muhar. He was followed as CO by Clyde E. Murr, probably the most outstanding CIC agent in Korea and Japan. He served with the 7th doing positive intelligence, handling 'line crossers,' and later became CO. He served 8 years in Japan and Korea, from Japan in some of the most secret operations of post WW2. A platoon sergeant in Italy WW2, and commissioned in field.

Not a member of NCICA but should be. He lives at 2946 Lantern Drive, Daytona Bch FL 32119. I meet him in Florida each March. The finest officer I ever met, one who came up thru the ranks and knew how to treat his agents." [He indeed belongs in NCICA. Thanks for more names of agents, now added to roster. Sphinx.]

Edward GORMAN, East Hampton NY:

"In CIC 'medals,' you mention CIC agents were warned there would be no medals. I never heard of it—it does seem odd. Why such a warning? Who issued it? Were my Bronze stars (Leyte; Okinawa) in error? My Purple Heart was for Okinawa 21 June 45; in Leyte, a field commission?" [Thank you for bringing this up, Ed. You earned every medal you got, and more, Ed. And many earned medals they did not get. The warning was verbal when I was sworn into CIP 24 December 1941, by Asa W Candler III in Atlanta. Was he in error? It certainly was not followed everywhere. Perhaps others might shed some light on this for us. Sphinx]

....

Ralph N HARKNESS, Tucson AZ:

"This is my address for 5 months; we return to 7740 N River Edge Dr, Milwaukee WI 53209 for Xmas and grandchildren. My reading GS has been 3-4 issues. The last one reminded me of a skinny 19 year old interpreter in Fulda we called 'Heinz' (Kissinger). Fulda, Kassel and Marburg were sub-offices of the Bad-Nauheim detachment. Sidney Jurin and I were in Kassel office. John Thatcher (Library of Congress career) broke the case of the English-speaking secretaries Russians trained to work in our installations; he interrogated one from Koenigsburg whose cover was her father was an MD in that community."

....

Ambassador Chic Hecht, Las Vegas NV [to our Chairman]:

"You were correct in replacing me on the Board. My wife and I have been spending a great amount of time in Europe. I plan to get involved in international business. I will make every effort to be in Chattanooga for the 50th. My best to all."

XXXI

Will Rogers, November 1929:
*New York hotel clerks ask guests signing in,
"Do you wanna room for sleeping or for jumping?"*

How Deep Was the Great Depression?

At the bottom [1932-3] to-wit:

Employment

ON AVERAGE: ONE OUT of every three or four employable workers was out of work in the US, in many places much higher. In one Southern Illinois county ALL able-bodied workers were unemployed; in some Appalachian mining cities only 200 to 300 out of thousands were still on the job. In Harlan County KY whole towns had NO income at all—people lived on dandelions and blackberries.

Many with jobs had salaries cut. In some public sectors like schools, teachers were paid only with scrip [promise in writing to pay, if and when]; some businesses accepted these in hopes of collecting. Lack of funds closed 2,600 elementary schools nationwide! Banks began to fail in large numbers. On 4 February 1933 Louisiana's governor, followed by others, closed ALL banks in the state for a time. President Roosevelt, elected in 1932, did the same nationwide to restore hope to Americans.

Sources of Assistance

President Hoover's theory: primary obligations rested on family, neighbors, landlord, employer—in that order. Next came local charities, and finally local government possibly assisted by state grants. Federal aid would undermine the "spirit of responsibility of states, municipalities, industry and the country at large." Local agencies were safer because subject to local control and less harmful to the recipient.

But an urban working family was unable to help its own when the breadwinner had no job; stricken neighbors were no better off. Some landlords realized it did no good to evict tenants with no replacements, and became lenient. Smaller businesses went under. Larger ones downsized, often reducing hours and sharing work. Least skilled were first to go; managers began to handle work done by employees. Some firms set up loan funds and other relief measures for former workers. ALL just a drop in the bucket.

Farmers generally could grow their own food but not sell it to people with no money; sharecroppers often subsisted on turnips as cotton was inedible. Sheep farmers cut the throats of young lambs and threw them in canyons; they were unable to feed them. Excess cattle met a similar fate in many areas.

Most small cities had NO relief programs. As for charities in larger cities, after private donors came voluntary organizations like Red Cross, Salvation Army, Community Chest. When these ran out of funds, only local and state appropriations could possibly help. "By the end of 1931, municipal relief—private and public—was bankrupt in virtually every city in the U.S." Unemployment rose 50 percent in the next 18 months.

Stop-Gap Measures

First steps toward a Welfare State were suggested in 1931 by Eugene Meyer Jr, a Hoover appointee to the Federal Reserve Board. It went against his ideals, but Hoover reluctantly agreed, believing it to be for the emergency only, and wouldn't set a precedent. December 1931 the federal RFC [Reconstruction Finance Corporation] was created to lend to needy businesses, and in July 1933 upped the amount to lend to needy states.

For hungry locals and travelers seeking work, soup kitchens and bread lines existed in larger cities, usually maintained by churches, charities and a few private citizens still with means. The food served varied from watery soup to more ample beans, probably scrounged from waste from nearby industries and farmers. Food was cheap and plentiful; if a dollar could be earned it would feed a family of four for three or four days. Crops that farmers could not sell for a profit rotted in the fields, unless passers-by seized the opportunity to pick a free meal.

Effect on Families

Thomas C. Cochran:

> "Breakdown of respect for parents and family sustenance, hope and security, had a serious impact on children brought up between 1929 and 1940."

Today's generations don't know how luckier they are than those in the early Great Depression years. There did not exist such crutches as unemployment benefits, guaranteed minimum wages, retirement benefits, federal student loan programs, health insurance, insured bank deposits, social security, Medicaid and Medicare, and HMOs [Health Maintenance Organizations]. Many other aids for those out of work came into existence during the Roosevelt years [1933-1945]: such as the CCC [Civilian Conservation Corps], the SBA [Small Business Administration] and the WPA [Work Projects Adm.], and a number of other remedies that I cannot begin to enumerate.

Before the Great Depression, most Americans were brought up to believe in the ideals pronounced by Hoover [he was an orphan]: you are responsible for yourself; the government did not owe you a living or even an opportunity to obtain one.

Thomas Cochran noted [above] a connection between the Great Depression and World War Two, but Caroline Bird completely ignored the WWII comparison when she wrote of the Great Depression: ".... it packed a bigger wallop than anything else that happened to America between the Civil War and the Atom Bomb."

The above information was gleaned while doing research for The Great Depression and a Teenager's Fight to Survive, *which contains six months of the author's experiences as a teenager living the life of a hobo in 1932-3, the very bottom of the Great Depression. The book may be obtained direct from Red Apple Publishing, 15010 - 113th St, KPN Gig Harbor 98329; 1-800/245-6595, or the author at 1421 Miner St. #617, Seattle, WA 98101 or Email: Goldsphinx@aol.com.*

This book reaped these honors:

- An invitation to speak at a Louisiana State University seminar for high school teachers in 1996.

- Selected by Arizona Governor's Advisory Counsel on Aging to appear at annual conference in Mesa AZ in 1996.

- American History Project in Brooklyn NY researching youths who rode boxcars in the Great Depression notified author this book was being sent to Smithsonian's Great Depression archives.

- Junior and senior high school and college teachers have stated this book is worth bringing to the attention of such students nationwide.

XXXII

Cactus Jack Y Canon—CIC *or Ranger*?

JACK Y CANON, MEXIA TX, graduated from San Antonio Public School of Law in 1935. A lawyer entering U.S. Army he became a CIP [Corps of Intelligence Police] Special Agent, attended DC CIP school and was a CIP officer by 1942. In 1942 Canon replaced the commanding officer in Houston TX CIC office. Experienced Special Agents Steve Davis and Jim Herrington were in the office. First thing Canon did was buy a high-powered rifle with a scope. Demonstrating it to the office staff he would say, "I'll use it to kill damned Japs."

One of Canon's first orders to Herrington was destroy an informant list Herrington had worked on for months. Later he accused Herrington of coming to work late, threatening him with dereliction of duty or being AWOL. The detachment was assigned one government car; one day it disappeared with Herrington being accused. He was innocent: he had his own car which he used in the business.

One day Herrington called in reporting a slight case of diarrhea prevented him working. Answering a knock on his door, medics with an ambulance confronted him, sent by Canon to take him to a hospital. It's doctors declared hospitalization unnecessary.

Early in the war CIC was ordered to keep an eye on anyone known or suspected of being Communist or sympathizer. Movie actor Melvin Douglas was in Houston's area awaiting a Captain's commission; Canon had him investigated as his U.S. Congresswoman wife was suspected of communist leanings. Douglas heard of it, picked up a phone and called Eleanor Roosevelt who got his commission quickly.

Canon Sent to Australia

Near end of 1943, Canon was ordered overseas. Reaching Ft Holabird, Baltimore MD, he found orders to report to SWPA HQ in Brisbane, Australia, along with Lt Earl Klein leading 13 special agents.

December 31st he and his men embarked on SS Matsonia, converted Hawaiian luxury liner, departing next morning unescorted by naval battleships. After 18 days zigging and zagging across the Pacific, it reached Brisbane, Australia.

After several weeks familiarizing with theatre setup, Canon found what he wanted: he got permission to head the first team assigned to a combat unit in SWPA, 41st Inf Div on New Guinea at Finschhaffen, training for Hollandia, Dutch New Guinea.

He picked for his SAC [Special Agent in Charge] Duval A Edwards. Duval came to Australia on the same ship and was SAC of Sydney CIC for a six month tour of duty. Edwards served six weeks when called to Brisbane HQ. On arriving he found orders putting him under Jack Y Canon, now known as Texas or Cactus Jack. Soon another 11 agents joined him. Lt Canon called them together to say they had two weeks to train for jungle. In uniforms with packs and weapons, training was day marches into Australia's outback under hot sun and cloudless sky, some days going twenty miles to get into physical shape.

At end of training, they boarded a plane across the strait to Port Moresby, New Guinea, spending one night there. Next morning they flew across peaks of Owen Stanley Mountains to Finschhaffen where they joined the 41st Division.

Getting settled by dark, Canon finally called Duval into his tent. Instead of a first-time conversation about the mission, Canon's only said "shine my shoes." Wondering if he should say that was not an SAC's job, Duval decided to comply silently.

Next morning Canon assigned each man to talk to a certain unit of the division on importance of turning in every scrap of paper with Japanese writing to ATIS [Allied Translators and Interpreters] to translate. Canon rarely talked with the unit or with any one individual, not even Duval who he had made his senior agent in charge.

Following intensive bombardment by Navy battleships at Hollandia, the first wave of soldiers landed. There was little gun-fire; the enemy had fled. Duval made it ashore in the third wave, reporting to Capt Coffey, 162 Regimental S-2.

Canon had assigned him there without any conversation or specific orders. He stayed with the 162 Regt for three days emptying a Japanese post-office, when agent David Lincoln from CIC at Division HQ came saying Canon badly needed him at HQ. Duval was only agent who spoke Pasar [low] Malay, Indonesian language where they were now. Reaching HQ, Duval saw Canon at a distance but started work speaking to natives in Malay, answering their questions. He finally reasoned this was why Canon had ordered him there, to keep them from pestering him; again Canon never talked with Duval.

With slight resistance Hollandia was over in thirty days. CIC then boarded an LST for Biak island up the coast. Again Canon was not present, leaving Duval in charge without saying a word to him. Reaching new target, following a massive fleet bombardment the agents went over LST's side into landing barges. With his regular pack Edwards carried his tommy gun, a .38, the unit typewriter, *plus Canon's rifle and pistol* [Canon never explained why]; heavily burdened he had trouble descending the ladder.

Division's leading elements headed up the beach to take Mokmer, nearest airfield but were stopped by heavy fire from enemy in caves hidden in cliffs bordering the beach.

Division HQ picked a grove of trees well away from the front. Except for agents assigned to fighting units, CIC did also. This situation lasted weeks as fighting was extremely heavy near the airfield. Duval set up the typewriter on a table under a tree, but found little to do. The agents lounged around the table waiting for Canon to direct activities.

At first Canon was gone for hours each day, supposedly looking for documents in vacated caves, but brought back souvenirs of all kinds—sabers, Japanese flags, rifles, etc. He was awarded a silver star for one day's work when he found some documents. At first he never asked an agent to go with him, nor did he ever ask Duval to get one.

Duval opened the single drawer in the table-desk one morning to find fire grenades. Canon had been dropping one behind agents at times, scaring daylights out of them. Duval returned the few from the desk to Canon explaining the desk was not safe.

Canon finally began calling on different agents to accompany him. The men first asked Duval if it was okay, telling Duval where the trip went. Sometimes he said, "It's okay." At other times he said it was an I and R platoon operation. Canon never commented on this countering his orders.

Days passed until a day Canon called Duval to his tent and said, "I'm sending you up front to replace the agent there."

Duval said "Yes sir," got his few belongings and headed

up the coast. He was at 186th Reg HQ for a month. A Japanese patrol was ambushed early one morning, leaving some 20 bodies he searched for writing. Afterwards, there was little to do as there were no bodies nor places with Japanese writing, and no natives to interrogate. Finally Mokmer airfield was liberated; U.S. planes started using it.

One day Duval was called back to CIC HQ. Canon said he was relieving him of duty and returning him to Brisbane for reassignment. Duval said goodbye to the men, headed to the airfield and next plane to Brisbane via Hollandia. Friends at CIC HQ told him Canon had sent an efficiency report on him showing zero across the board, whereas following Hollandia operation he had received excellent marks. After vacationing in Sydney, Duval was visited by Capt Marvin Goff, CO of 214th CIC, XIV Corps, questioning him extensively. At the end, Goff stated, "I knew of Canon back in Texas. To me a zero efficiency rating from Canon is a high mark. Would you like to be my SAC?" Duval said yes – so instead of being kicked out of CIC, he was on his way to a new assignment in Bougainville, Soloman Islands.

Next word of Canon was a month later when he heard Canon had arrested Alajajian, one of Duval's agents in 41st, for disobeying a direct order in a combat area and was to be court-martialed in Brisbane. Guilty verdict meant death. Duval, fearing his counter orders influenced the agent, immediately wrote Alajajian offering to testify in his behalf, It was not needed as the court martial committee decreed the charge was not justified; Alajajian went to another CIC unit earning two medals on Luzon.

It was not until after the war that Duval learned: Alajajian went on prior patrols with Canon but got word his brother in Boston had died. Upset, he asked to be excused. Canon insisted but he still refused, then Canon had him arrested and returned handcuffed to Brisbane for trial. Canon was also at the trial.

When Court dismissed charge, all stepped up to congratulate Alajajian, ignoring Canon.

In Japan after the War

One agent sent to Tokyo area reported one day as he was transporting Canon to a nearby office Canon sat with a shotgun shooting randomly in the air. He headed a new unit to secure positive intelligence on enemy activity. Russia flooded agents to convert Japan to communism. Unit initials was SOB, adequately describing Texas Jack Canon, who should never have been in CIC.

After the Korean conflict he was kicked out of CIC to the MPs, stationed at Ft Hood TX. Charged with shooting cattle on a nearby ranch, he was arrested and imprisoned at Ft Sam Houston TX. Mutual friend Blair Labatt persuaded Duval to visit him. He presented Canon with a carton of Canon's favorite cigarettes, receiving a surly "Thanks." That ended the meeting. Canon escaped punishment by producing copies of orders showing he was far away on the date of the alleged crime.

Arthur Hurlburt, a friend of Duval's, years later said that Canon was under suspicion of contacting enemy agents. Hurlburt tailed him for two days to see who he might contact. Canon, apparently aware of being tailed, never made contact. Hurlburt was relieved of duty and saw Canon no more.

Years later, a story in a Japanese newspaper reported Canon's death by suicide in his home town of Mexia. Translated, it reported great dislike of Japanese people for Canon and relief at his death.